The

Ellingtons

BY:

JUSTICE LOVE

Revised Edition

ISBN-13:
978-1518642357

ISBN-10:
1518642357

Dedicated to anyone who believe their dreams are unobtainable. Just reach, por qua pa (why not), it's right there. This book has been in my dreamology world for a long time, and now it is here. Never stop dreaming no matter what.

I would like to acknowledge my personal Lord and Savior, Jesus Christ, because without Him I am truly nothing.

I want to acknowledge the two best, beautiful and hilarious sisters a girl could ever have, Rachell and Tameka.

Dennis Sr. and Carol, I think all the deities got together and decided to overdose me with laughter and love, then they put me in your care. Thank you for listening to my rants that didn't make sense. Thank you for the gentle guiding that kept me on the right path.

Dad you always taught me that I can have and do what I want, I believed you and the accomplishments are still growing.

Mom you always tell me not to borrow trouble, I'm still working on that one.

MS thank you for always trying to hold me down, I look forward to my daily triumphs over you.

Thank you God and family because I live a wonderful life.

THE ELLINGTONS: *how the saga began*

A story that explores how problems do not respect social status. This is a tale of a twisted saga that will cause you to experience a plethora of emotions. Just when you think you know, you discover that you do not know.

Welcome to the world of *The Ellingtons*.

Happy reading...words are wonderful

Justice Love

Antonia,

Thank you for the love and support. I love you bunches.

Justice love

love:

"Honey wake up." Sean whispered in Halcyon's ear. She did not respond. Sean got real close to her ear lobe and rubbed it with the tip of his nose and then he tried his request again with a softer whisper, "it's time to wake up sweetheart."

This attempt got him an ever so gentle smile and pleasurable, "Mmmm...." Halcyon then adjusted her head on her pillow so that she was facing Sean and she asked in a sleepy and groggy voice, "Do I really have to wake up?"

At that point Halcyon heard another woman's voice. Halcyon tried to figure out whose voice she was hearing because it did not match the female voices in her immediate memory bank. She opened her eyes and her surroundings were not familiar to her. Panic began to set in as she tried to get eye contact with Sean. The woman's voice was still talking and Halcyon was not paying attention to the woman's words. Halcyon needed Sean's attention. Where was she? As she studied Sean's face for comfort, she felt a hand touch her shoulder very gently. She turned around to see who was touching her and there she saw a sweet, comforting face staring back at her smiling.

Then the woman said, "I apologize for waking you, but we will be landing in approximately twenty minutes. I need you to put your seat back in its upright position."

Halcyon smiled back at the flight attendant and let out a sigh of relief. Man she was extremely exhausted, she was on her way to her honeymoon destination and she was momentarily oblivious to everything. She sat up in her seat, crossed her legs, and wedged her left hand between her thighs. Something on her hand scratched her leg through her linen pants. She looked to see if she damaged her pants and noticed the new wedding band sitting just below the engagement ring that housed the large diamond on her ring finger. She admired her wedding band for a moment. She took a deep breath and a hard swallow and whispered, "We finally did it. I am finally Mrs. Spencer."

Then Sean whispered responding as he gently rubbed her cheek with the back of his fingers, "I would have waited forever."

She knew he was telling the truth, she was so satisfied with them loving one another.

They exchanged "I love you," and shared a kiss so passionate that everything ceased to exist to salute their love for one another.

When the plane landed, it taxied into the Ellington hub where a town car and stretch limousine waited their arrival. When they got off of the plane Halcyon walked out of the hub to take in the scenery. She never thought that she would be back in Holland on her honeymoon. As she looked around Sean walked up behind her and hugged her waist. He kissed the back of her neck. She turned to face him and got butterflies in her stomach. His palms became sweaty. He was her gentleman and she was his lady; they pledged to love one another forever. Sean took a step away from Halcyon and asked if he could have this dance. Halcyon could not stop smiling and with a simple nod of her head and a simultaneous blink of her eyes, she accepted his request, even though there was no dance floor or music to accompany them. Love was the flawless track that knitted their hearts together.

He put his left hand out and she placed her right hand in his left hand.

Their gaze never left one another's.

With his right hand he placed it around her waist, guiding her body ever so gently into his own.

Her left hand rested on his right shoulder.

"Thank you for bringing me back here," she said in a whisper.

"I would do anything for you," he responded in the same whisper.

Halcyon laid her head on his shoulder and she said, "You make me all giddy inside."

"You make me feel like I can do anything," he responded.

Then she said "I can't believe how good I feel when I am with you."

"I can't believe how much I miss you when you are not by my side," he responded. Then he said, "Halcyon I just love you, it's that simple for me."

She kissed him on the neck, took another deep breath and she began to sing the words: "...for all we know this may only be a dream. We come and we go like the ripples on a stream, so love me tonight. Tomorrow was made for some, tomorrow may never come for all we know."

Then they stood still and held each other for what seemed like an eternity.

one:

Hannah's eyes opened, for no reason at all from a deep sleep. She rolled over and her alarm clock caught her attention as the time of 4:30 a.m. glared back into her tired eyes. The flashing blue light on her cell phone flirted with her consciousness and forced her to curse under her breath. She picked up the cell phone and tried to read the screen but her eyes had no intention of focusing. Suddenly the urge to use the bathroom became overwhelming. She went to the bathroom then walked back to the bed and sat on its edge, and then she thought, *I'm not going back to sleep*.

She picked up her cell phone and attempted to read the screen again and she said in a reprimanding whisper, *Why did you have to ring at 4:28 in the morning and record a message?*

She punched in the code to her voicemail with much attitude to find out who was trying to get in touch with her at this insane hour IN THE MORNING! When she heard the voice that was recorded, she began to smile and all of the anger of inconvenience immediately left. While she was still listening to the message she decided to go into the family kitchen and have a cup of herbal tea. When Hannah got to the bottom of the bottom of the stairs she noticed that the kitchen light was on and she heard a sniffle or two. She instantly knew that it was her mother.

While she walked into the kitchen, Hannah activated the voicemail again. Then she walked over to her mother whose back was turned to her and said, "Mudear, here. Press two and listen." She handed her mother the phone and walked over to the stove to check the kettle for water.

She filled the kettle, put it on the stove, turned on the stove, and faced her mother to read her expression.

Mudear then closed the phone and took a deep breath of satisfaction. She forced a smile and handed the phone back to Hannah. She reached out to hug her mother and whispered in her ear, "Are you okay now?"

Mudear gave Hannah an extra squeeze, let her go and looked at her adoringly. Then Mudear said, "I think all three of my daughters are trying to put me in an early grave."

Hannah just smiled and continued to listen. Although, she did make a mental note to herself that her mother said three and not four daughters. Her mother just disowned a child, interesting. Oh how my sisters and I would fight over such a coveted position.

"I'm not trying to be in anyone's business, I just

want to know that the destinations have been reached, that's all," Mudear continued.

"It's okay; you heard Cy's voice yourself. They are okay," Hannah said, trying to defend her baby sister.

Hannah understood why her mother was so upset. When Mudear was a child her mother traveled a lot because she was involved with numerous charities. When Mudear was five years old she got the chicken pox and was unable to travel with her mother. Before her mother left on the next trip she promised Mudear that she would only be gone for a few hours and that she would call her when she landed. There was a malfunction with the plane and it went down over the ocean. The next time Mudear saw her mother was at her funeral, and she never called like she promised. To this day Mudear gets unnerved whenever her immediate family is traveling by plane, which is why three of her four children chose to live in Atlanta. McKenzie chose to live in New York partly for that same reason, to unnerve her mother every time she traveled by plane.

Hannah sat down at the kitchen table drinking her herbal tea, while Mudear drank some hot apple cider.

"Hannah Joe," Mudear began and Hannah looked at her mother with undivided attention, "how did you know what was wrong with me?"

Hannah was a little surprised by the question but she decided to entertain her mother so she answered, "Well if you consider the content of Cy's message and couple that with your feelings about us flying, I just drew a simple conclusion."

"What if you were wrong?" Mudear said matter of factly.

"Then I would have been wrong, right?" Hannah questioned with a very even tone voice as she tried to figure out where Mudear was going with this conversation.

"You do realize that sometimes you are wrong and you do not always have the right answer for everything?" Mudear was looking for an argument.

Hannah fingered the rim of the tea mug as she put thoughts together before she answered and then said, "I am very aware that I am Hannah and not The Omniscient One. Because I *DO NOT know* what you are doing here, I'm just gonna bow out gracefully."

"Just because you are 28 years old, doesn't mean you can sass me."

Hannah threw her hands up in surrender. Mudear cut her own words off as Hannah's action disturbed her.

Then she asked her becoming extremely upset through tight lips, "Why did you put your hands up like that?"

Hannah made a mental note of Mudear's response before she answered and then said, "Sass you? Oh yeah. Hands up. I forfeit. I surrender because I do not know the rules that have been set for this game you are trying to play. You win."

"That's not funny."

"And I'm not laughing."

"Let me ask you something."

Hannah knew she should have ended the conversation but her curiosity got the best of her so she said with great reservation, "Okay."

"Are you looking for another Anthony?" Mudear asked very nonchalantly.

Hannah wanted to say, *really bitch*, just as nonchalantly as the question was asked, but her mouth responded politely with, "No mam."

"Then what are you looking for?" Mudear seemed so distant mentally right now.

"The answer to why you just bit off my head. Also, why on earth did you bring up Anthony of all people?" Hannah was tired and annoyed. Then she said to herself, *you are having a conversation with an unreasonable person, DON'T ask another question.*

Mudear was lost in space and Hannah was about to

try and sneak out of the kitchen.

Then Mudear said, "I am still angry with Presscott."

The mention of her oldest sister's name awakened her. That was an argument that she wanted to have with her mother. Hannah took a long thoughtful drink of her tea. She looked at her mother with no emotion on her face, she cleared her throat and then the interrogation began:

"What's going on with you and Scottie?"

"What do you mean?"

"Why can't you say anything nice to her?"

"I don't say nice things to people I don't like."

"You are referencing to your first born." Then Hannah thought, *am I really having this conversation?*

"So."

"Is that all you have to say?"

"I personally think that I tolerate Presscott pretty well."

"Yeah, I'm starting to take this personal."

"Why?"

"Normally mothers love their children, not just tolerate them. She is 32 years old, not 2."

"And your point?"

"Do you realize how much pain you cause her?"

"Again your point is? I don't care."

"Well that's the understatement of the century."

"What are you implying Hannah Joe?"

"You had to grow up without your mother due to a physical death, and Scottie had to grow up without her mother due to an emotional detachment by choice of her mother.

"That's enough."

"What did she ever do to deserve a mother like you?"

"That's enough."

"When was the last time that you told her that you loved her?"

"I believe I said that's enough Hannah."

"It is enough, but I do wonder how many times you told her that when she was a child."

"If I don't love someone why would I say so?"

"You would make a great psychological case study."

"What is your point?"

"Earlier you stated that you had three children, has it finally come to Scottie not even existing in your world?"

"I truly do understand that I gave birth to Presscott but I wish it wasn't so."

"Mudear seek help because you have some serious

issues that need to be worked out. If you are not careful you will lose your other three children by default. And since we are talking, understand we are not children anymore. Your youngest child got married two days ago and she is twenty six."

Hannah decided that was all she had to say to her mother. Silent tears of fury were running down her face as she tried to process the conversation with her mother. Hannah placed her mug in the kitchen sink and began to walk into the hallway.

Mudear stood blocking the entrance of the kitchen with her hands on her hips and said, "Hannah Joe you will not use that tone with me."

Hannah cut her mother's words off in a soft voice, "Or what? Then I could be banished to the land of motherless children. Maybe that would be best."

Mudear was taken aback by Hannah's words. Her eyes began to plead with Hannah, "Okay, that's enough from both of us," she said in a very consoling voice.

Finally something Hannah could agree with and then she added to her mother's statement, "For now it is enough, but please understand that this is nowhere near from being over."

Hannah's thoughts were all over the place. One decision she did make was to call for the Johnson mansion to be prepared for her to move back in.

Mudear interrupted Hannah with a gentle touch on her arm and said, "You never answered my question."

Hannah turned to face her mother and with closed eyes and through mental exhaustion she said, "What is it now Mudear?"

Mudear had never seen her daughter that upset and took a step back as she studied her face and then she continued with her question, "Do you think you will ever get married again?"

Why bitch why? Was the question she thought in her head but she absolutely would not resolve to disrespecting her mother, so she simply said, "Wow," with pure astonishment on her face.

"Wow? Wow is not the response I was looking for," she said tilting her head forward as if she were looking over a pair of glasses.

Hannah then mentally turned on the teacher from the Charlie Brown voice recorder in her head because she did not want to hear anything else that her mother had to say.

Mudear followed her determined to get her bid in on her daughter's next date.

Hannah was getting further away from the sound of

her mother's voice but she did hear her say, "Corbin Wolfe...attorney at your firm." Then the Charlie Brown voice recorded kicked back in.

As she carefully pulled away from her mother the only thing that could comfort her now was a slow scenic drive to Pesscott's house.

It was 5:15 in the morning and Hannah really wanted to be asleep and she needed to be near her sister. She crossed over to highway 78 from highway 285, drove past Stone Mountain, cruised through Decatur and into Midtown.

Hannah knew her brother-in-law was out of town so she went straight to Presscott's bedroom and crawled into bed with her. Presscott rolled over to face her sister and asked in a whisper, "Do we need to talk about it now?"

Hannah cleared her throat and simply said, "No," as a single tear made a path across the bridge of her nose.

Presscott reached for the tissue box from her night stand and wiped the tear from her sister's nose and said, "Han whatever this is we will get through it, okay?" Presscott then kissed Hannah on the forehead and watched her until she fell asleep.

To Presscott this smelled just like Mudear, which

also meant that her name was tangled in this mess. Needless to say, Presscott did not sleep the rest of the night.

Presscott prayed.

She first prayed for McKenzie. McKenzie was the second child born to the Ellingtons and she was a fireball. She spoke her mind and did not care how it came out. She was the one that lived in New York because her passion was dancing. She had her own dance studio there and doing well, so it seemed. McKenzie was staying with Presscott while she was in town because she didn't like Mudear at all and didn't hide that fact.

Next Presscott prayed for Halcyon, the Interior Designer, her baby sister who just got married. She was proud of her. Halcyon learned at an early age to always be cordial and move on. Halcyon had extremely tough skin, but was always the gentle southern belle in public; never willing to embarrass anyone publicly.

Finally Presscott prayed for Hannah, the attorney that was trapped in the grief of the death of her husband, Anthony. After Anthony died, Hannah was no longer present; she was always somewhere else mentally. Presscott gave Hannah a lot of hugs and kisses just to reassure her that she was not alone. Presscott knew there was nothing she could do, say or give to Hannah to make her heart stop hurting, but she did understand the power of the human touch and time. Whenever Presscott and Hannah were in a room together, Presscott always made sure that Hannah was within arm's length away and she constantly told Hannah that she loved her.

These were Presscott's three sisters that helped her stay connected as an Ellington.

two:

After Sean and Halcyon got married Jonathan had to leave town for some business meetings in D.C. Presscott chose not to go on this trip because her younger sister, McKenzie was in town staying with her. Besides, if Presscott started to miss Jonathan she would just get on a plane and fly to him. Four days had passed since the wedding and Presscott wondered how her baby sister was holding up. Presscott was so impressed with Halcyon and was aware that the youngest child in the family was a big girl now, but still, the big sister wanted to make sure everything was okay.

Even though Presscott was concerned about her baby sister her thoughts went to missing Jonathan. She kept feeling like she was going to really need him today and she could not figure out why. She looked around for a distraction, noticed the time and decided that McKenzie needed to be awakened. She called McKenzie on the intercom system but she did not answer. Then Presscott walked into the vast hallway and began to re-evaluate why she and Jonathan needed a mansion. She was at the end of the East Wing and McKenzie was one floor up at the end of the West Wing. A profane word was the thought that Presscott had because she was tired from her workout that her trainer had just put her through. She called one of the workers to see the trainer out and she began the five minute jog to McKenzie but then quickly decided to Free Run the distance. She wanted to work on getting height for a Wall Gainer. So she ran to a closed door as hard as she could. She planted her right foot on the door with great force and the door flung open. She soared through the air and tried to grab the door frame to prevent a horrible collision. Her momentum was moving faster than her thoughts and she crashed into an oversized Cherry Wood king size bed. The impact of her body into the bed was equivalent to hitting a brick wall full speed. She jumped up immediately and fell right back down on the bed. She laid there and laughed at herself for a moment. She regained her composure and walked to McKenzie.

She thought she was going to die by the time she got to McKenzie so she yelled out to her, "Hey Sleeping Beauty, are you going to wake up today?"

McKenzie looked at the clock to see what time it was, "11:45, why is she up so early?" she mumbled the question to herself.

Then McKenzie heard this continual soft annoying knock on the door and then her sister began to sing, "*Way up in sky the little birds fly...*"

McKenzie put the pillow over her head to try and block out her singing.

"...*way down in the nest the little birds rest.*"

McKenzie rolled over and thought, *she has got to be kidding.*

"...*with the wings on the left and wings the wings on the right...*"

McKenzie was about to lose it. She could not believe that her sister was doing this to her.

"...*the little birds rest way down in the nest...*"

McKenzie decided to get up because she was wide awake now thanks to her big sister. "Okay Scottie I'm up damn it!" she yelled at her sister.

"Did you just cuss at me younger sister of mine?" Presscott asked in a playful voice as she opened the door.

"Yes I did." McKenzie answered her in a serious staccato voice.

"Well I'm sorry for waking you up 15 minutes before noon but you do not want to be late for brunch with *your* mother at Phipps Plaza."

Then McKenzie remembered that the monthly brunch with her mother and sisters was still on even though Halcyon was on her honeymoon. "Shit Scottie I forgot all about that, give me a few minutes."

"Kennie slow down, I moved the time back to 1:30, so you have some time." Presscott said as she gently put a hand on her sister's wrist to pull her back down on the bed next to her.

"I have to take a shower, please let me go." McKenzie had been stand offish towards her family ever since she got into town for the wedding.

"Are you going to tell me what's wrong or are you going to be miserable the entire month that you are here?" Presscott never believed in beating around the bush with her patients and she was not about to start with her family.

"Nothing is wrong with me…"Presscott cut off McKenzie before she could finish her statement with, "Younger sister of mine you know I don't do well with people lying to me so I am just going to assume that you want to be miserable." Presscott got up to walk out of the room and when she got to the door she had an impulse to turn around. She looked at her tough acting sister who could handle anything in her own way sitting on the edge of the bed with the posture of defeat. Without saying a word Presscott walked back over to the bed and hugged her younger sister. When McKenzie felt Presscott's touch the floodgates of her heart burst opened followed by uncontrollable sobs. Presscott just held on to her silently to reassure them both that they were going to get through this matter together whatever it was. McKenzie cried for what seemed like an eternity but never once did Presscott indicate restlessness. When McKenzie finished crying Presscott walked over to the bathroom and got some wet wipes and Advil for the killer headache that her sister was bound to have.

McKenzie took a deep breath and as she released it she said, "I had an abortion."

Presscott was not prepared for this one. Being a Psychologist kept Presscott on her feet at all times but these four words were an unexpected sucker punch to the abdomen. Presscott was deflated but she dare not show that to her sister so she just simply said, "I love you so much younger sister of mine."

"I don't get it Doc," McKenzie started, "Aren't you disappointed in me? Aren't you mad at me? After all we were taught that if we had an abortion we would burn in hell for murder."

Presscott smiled at her sister and said, "That's a scare tactic used to try and stop girls from having unwanted pregnancies. That never works. Besides, no words or actions from me can beat you up worse than you have already obviously done to yourself. What has happened, happened. It will never make me love you less."

This is what made all of Presscott's sisters run to her when they had a problem. Everything seemed to make her love them more and she was never condescending. This was also why Mudear was only respected as the one who had the womb to carry the four sisters.

Near the end of her relationship McKenzie noticed that Michael had put distance between the two of them. She wanted to figure out how to confront him so she decided one random night to dance out her thoughts and concerns in her studio. In keeping with her normal routine, when she walked into the dance studio she checked all of her *IN* boxes. The fourteen year old jazz class had a song for her to approve, "Kennie our class would like to change one of our numbers to 'Curious' by 3LW #8 on the CD. - Shauna" Shauna was one of her success stories and now she was an assistant dance instructor.

McKenzie walked into her private dance room and put on the CD. The song immediately made her think about what was going on between her and Michael. She walked over to the CD player and programmed the song to repeat and she pushed the play button again and then heard a noise that caught her attention. Sammy, her head bodyguard, stepped into the room and asked if she was okay. She nodded an affirmative nod with a quizzical look on her face. They both decided to find out what the noise was and as they walked through the building they could hear the noises in rhythmic sets. They turned down the main hall and noticed a dim light shining through one of the dance rooms and realized that the noise was coming from the room of the light source. Sammy got to the door first, drew his gun and prepared to shoot. When Sammy realized what was happening, he dropped his gun and looked at McKenzie very disappointedly. McKenzie walked up to him with a look of befuddlement and then she noticed a trail of clothes leading to the table in the corner of the room. The sight of the clothes made her smile to herself because she thought, *you never get busted by your boss getting it in at work.*

She looked up at the table to see who she was going to have a talk with and there she saw Michael and Shauna having sex on the table. The noise in rhythmic sets was the table knocking against the mirrored wall. McKenzie's eyes filled with tears but not one drop escaped from them. She walked from the room hastily and delicately quiet. She went back to her studio and began to pace back and forth as she tried to get her thoughts together. Her heart was literally hurting in her chest and the simple act of breathing was laborious and becoming too much to handle. She took note that Sammy was watching her carefully from the doorway and she briskly began to turn off all of the equipment.

As she left the studio she aimlessly started giving Sammy instructions, "Please call The Ellington Gate and let them know that I need to fly to Nova Scotia in an hour. I would like a convertible Jag just like mine on the tarmac when I arrive. I want a copy of tonight's surveillance tape delivered to the cottage tomorrow. I don't believe that I will need a maid. I want that table delivered to Michael's house tomorrow afternoon. Let the school know that I will be gone for a week. I want Michael's access cards to my building, my apartment, and parking garage deactivated, under no circumstances is Michael to know my whereabouts. I need a gun with blanks in it. I think that's it."

Sammy looked at McKenzie ambiguously and followed her to the parking garage. Sammy walked over to his truck, turned back to face McKenzie and asked, "Do you want an automatic weapon or a hand gun?"

The tears refused to escape the boundaries of her eyes even though she answered with a quiver in her throat, "Automatic."

Sammy switched out the ammunition and gave her the automatic weapon and watched her storm back into the dance studio. He walked over to her car and drove it to the entrance she would exit out of then he heard the weapon sound off. Sammy had to laugh because of this kind of interruption during sex. *A woman scorned is nothing to play with.*

McKenzie walked through the entrance rubbing her chest with one hand and carrying the gun in the other. Tears tried to cleverly maneuver past her eye lids but she was too stubborn to let them fall and her breathing became shallow and dry. She got in the car and asked Sammy to call the police to let them know what she just did.

While he drove he made all of the proper arrangements according to her request and then proceeded to the airport. He parked her Jag next to the plane and then helped her with the door and her purse. Sammy would fly to Nova Scotia with her and fly back two days later just to make sure things were okay.

When McKenzie arrived in Nova Scotia, she became extremely sick. She thought that she was just upset about the latest turn of events but it was day number three and she was very sick to her stomach every morning. Sammy took it upon himself to call the family doctor to the cottage. That's when she found out that she was four weeks pregnant. McKenzie fell into a deep depression and her week trip turned into three weeks. She crawled into a corner of her bedroom and would not move except to answer sudden calls to go to the bathroom. She hated her life and could not figure out how to get out of it.

Finally, one morning McKenzie walked out of her bedroom for the first time and announced to Sammy that she wanted to fly back to New York that evening. She then requested that Michael be on the tarmac when she arrived because she had decisions that needed to be made.

As they drove to the airport McKenzie asked Sammy, "I still love him. Do you think I'm stupid?"

"No," he answered as if it were an obvious answer.

McKenzie wanted to inquire a little bit more so she asked him, "What do you think about all of this?" She became very passive as she took in the scenery for the first and last time of this trip.

Sammy's jaw tightened and then he answered, "I think that it's unfortunate for the baby."

McKenzie agreed with him in her thoughts and the rest of the ride was in silence.

When McKenzie got off of the plane in New York

and she saw Michael standing by her Jag. He tried to give her a hug and a kiss but she very politely discouraged him. She explained to him immediately what the doctor discovered and he became enraged. He accused her of getting pregnant to trap him to stay in the relationship. He explained to her that he wanted nothing to do with her any more. He asked her not to expect him to be a father to the baby. He questioned if the child was his and he did not want his name on the birth certificate.

She stood there quietly and listened to him rant and rave and when he was done, without looking at him she simply said, "Understood."

McKenzie got in her car and went home with silent rage festering in her very being. The next day she got the abortion and things were back to business as usual, so she thought.

Halcyon's wedding took place three and a half months after the abortion. She never discussed the affair, but McKenzie did mail a copy of the tape to Shauna's parents with a post it note on it that simply read, "The male in this video is Michael Owens, he taught Tap at The Ellington School of Dance. Mr. Owens has been terminated."

Presscott could not believe that her sister went through all of that by herself. How on earth did McKenzie maintain her sanity? "Well younger sister of mine, did you get a fine for disturbing the peace in the city."

"$150.000.00, a night in jail and two weeks of community service. I should invoice him huh?"

The sisters' conversation was interrupted by a soft tone from the intercom system then a gentle voice spoke, "Dr. Chandler I apologize for the disturbance but I have your sister Hannah holding on line one for you."

Presscott and McKenzie looked at the clock simultaneously and one said "shit" while the other one said "damn."

Presscott took a deep breath and said to the voice on the intercom, "You're not disturbing us. Martha, go ahead and put her through on the intercom."

A very short moment passed and Hannah's voice could be heard, "Hey Scottie, are you there?" Presscott and McKenzie smiled at one another because they knew this call was a cry for help.

Presscott answered with a little chuckle in her voice, "Yeah I'm here and Kennie is standing right next to me." McKenzie hit her sister on the shoulder playfully.

"Hey Kennie, Scottie please tell me that you guys are walking out the door right now."

"What's wrong Hannah?" McKenzie felt the need to ask the antagonizing question.

"Well if I put it nicely, Mudear is driving me crazy." Hannah answered extremely irritated.

"Wait. Where are you?" Presscott asked adorning a smile on her face.

"With Mudear," Hannah sounded flustered as her voice began to rise.

"By the way we need to talk Hannah Joe." Presscott, the mother said.

"Yes ma'am, we will talk but in the meantime can you help me now?" Hannah was pleading apologetically.

"Okay Han I hear you." Presscott's brain immediately went into action as she asked, "What is your exact location?"

Sounding a little distracted Hannah answered, "We just pulled into Phipp's Plaza."

Presscott was shooing McKenzie to go get dressed while she was talking to Hannah, "Mudear's favorite Gucci shop is on the bottom floor, if you take her in there you won't have to entertain the conversation about me and she will be more than preoccupied."

"Thank you, thank you." Hannah said with great appreciation.

"Don't thank me yet #3, can you very discreetly and in a nut shell tell me what happened to you the other night?"

"No I'm having brunch with my family right now so I will give you a call when I get done here. Thank you for checking in on me and we will be talking real soon." That was how Hannah answered Presscott.

"I understand. Railroad immediately following brunch," Presscott said with a maternal edge to her voice.

"Okay, until then," Hannah said soberly and then pressed 'end' on her cell phone.

Presscott yelled to McKenzie to meet her at the Escalade in ten minutes. Fifteen minutes later they were driving down the driveway on their way to Phipp's Plaza.

three:

On the first morning of her honeymoon Halcyon woke up, Sean was not in the bed with her. She thought he could have been in the bathroom, but when she got up to look he was not there. She washed her face and brushed her teeth. She threw her hair in a lazy pony tail on top of her head and tussled her bangs with her fingertips. She then removed the fake eyelashes from her real ones and took a step back and said, "Good morning Mrs. Spencer," with a simple pleasant smile.

Dressed in only Sean's pajama top, some biker shorts that zipped on both sides, and a pair of ankle socks, she began her quest to find her new husband.

When she reached the midpoint of the staircase her quest ended; she saw Sean fast asleep on the couch and he looked so uncomfortable. When she got to the bottom of the stairs she opened a closet door and took out an extra blanket and pillow. She walked over to the couch and very quietly placed the pillow on the coffee table. Sean stirred a little and Halcyon held her breath and stood very still so she would not wake him. Once Sean got still again she began to lay the blanket over him but suddenly stopped, Halcyon was taken aback as she noticed his pecks and abs. She reached out to just touch his chest softly because she wanted to make sure this was real. As her out stretched hand got closer to his chest it began to shake just a little and she slowly let her reach retract into herself. She stood watching him for a moment to etch his peaceful sleeping face in her memory and then she covered him with the blanket. She gently tucked the pillow between his head and the arm of the couch. As she walked through the doorway that connected the living room to the kitchen she turned around and leaned against the doorpost to get one last look at her sleeping beauty and then she whispered, "I love you."

She then busied herself making a cup of tea and returned to the upstairs bedroom. There she made herself comfortable in the bay window that overlooked a sea of Salmon colored tulips. She relived the details of her wedding and made a mental note to have a talk with Mudear when she returned to the states. Then she became very proud as she thought of the dance she had with her father. She recalled being nervous because she did not know if she would remember all of the steps, but she did and it was beautiful. Then she hugged her legs to her chest and rested her head on one knee. She allowed her thoughts to explore what was truly in her heart and she became excited about her future with Sean. The next thing she noticed was Sean sitting next to her with his back leaning against the window.

He traced the side of her face with the back of his fingertips and ushered her mind back to the present. She opened her eyes and he asked with a smile in his voice, "Was I there?"

The smirk at the corner of her lips answered the question but she followed the smile with a declaration in a whisper, "You are so beautiful."

"Humph...I think you are on the gorgeous side yourself." They both gave one another a seductive smile.

He leaned into her and they gave one another a good morning kiss. From there they went into a conversation that was absolutely meaningless. Neither one of them wanted to move, they were both trying to make the moment last forever.

Then Halcyon asked, "Do I sleep wild?"

Sean was a little puzzled by the question, so he answered with a question, "Why do you ask?"

She adjusted herself so that her back was against the window as well and she said, "When I woke up this morning you were not in the bed with me, why?"

"Ooohh," he replied and explained his actions. His father taught him that you never get in the bed with a lady unless you are invited.

four:

While Presscott and McKenzie drove to Phipp's Plaza they bobbed and bounced to the "Addicted" CD by Missy Elliot. As usual, Presscott had to fast forward the CD to number nine and she made the suggestion that McKenzie use the song for her older hip-hop class. They both displayed serious looks on their faces as the music played and then out of the blue McKenzie asked, "Why were you and Mudear fighting at the wedding?"

Presscott turned down the music, took a deep breath and explained what happened. McKenzie was appalled. McKenzie then said in a very monotone voice, "Because you gave her something borrowed huh...you two have to put an end to all of this and I have every intention of getting to the bottom of this today."

McKenzie's statement did not set too well with Presscott. Mudear intimidated Presscott and the truth was she just wanted to have a nice peaceful brunch with her mother and sisters.

They had a lot of details to figure out for Spencer Manor before Sean and Halcyon returned from Holland. Presscott became so consumed with her sister's last four words, "bottom of this today," that the rest of the ride was in silence.

THE BRUNCH:

When McKenzie and Presscott walked into the Gucci shop, Mudear was making her final purchase. Her items were then given to an assistant to make sure they were taken to the car.

Presscott was the first to speak, "Hello ladies, I apologize for our tardiness." Presscott then proceeded to give Hannah and Mudear a hug and a kiss.

McKenzie and Hannah exchanged looks of bewilderment because Presscott never showed affection towards Mudear.

Mudear was dumbfounded.

Then Presscott continued on with her thoughts, "Well are we ready to eat?"

There was still no hint of hostility or sarcasm and Mudear was about to explode.

The other two sisters braced themselves for Mudear's reaction and they went along as if everything were normal.

Once they were seated in the private dining room, Mudear immediately began to question Presscott's actions. As Mudear sat on the edge of her overstuffed chair, with her legs crossed at the ankles and both hands resting neatly on one knee she asked Presscott with great articulation, "Why on earth did you kiss and hug me in the Gucci store?"

Presscott's stomach began to turn and she suddenly felt all of the moisture in her mouth evaporate. Then she answered with as much courage as she could muster at that moment and said, "I was just happy to see you and it was my way of telling you that I would like to call a truce." With that said Presscott leaned toward the table and picked up her glass of water.

As she drank the water McKenzie noticed that Presscott's eyes were getting glassy. This was a response that McKenzie had never seen before. These were not tears, this was pure anger and she could not read Presscott's thoughts in her face. McKenzie reached under the table and placed a comforting hand on Presscott's leg and then desperately tried to change the subject by saying, "Now that we have that out of the way, we need to figure out when to meet over at Spencer Manor."

Mudear was still perched on the edge of the overstuffed chair as she said, "Yes we do need to figure out all of those details but I am not done speaking with your sister yet."

At that moment the waitress entered into the dining room to take their drink orders. Everyone ordered Some type of wine, except Presscott. She remained with her traditional water with no ice.

A heavy quietness fell over the room and Mudear broke the silence once the waitress was completely out of the dining room. "Let us understand something Presscott, you and I will never be happy to see one another. Now what exactly are you calling a 'truce' about?"

After Presscott took a drink of water her stomach subsided and she had an abundance of confidence when she answered Mudear audibly, "I would like for us to call a 'truce' on everything. I no longer want to argue with you because it is always about something that has nothing to do with the argument. I don't know what the 'something' is and that leaves me without the proper ability to oppose or agree. You are my mother and I am your daughter, can we just be that?"

McKenzie and Hannah looked at one another with astonishment and then they both turned to Mudear for her response.

Mudear sat back off of her perch and placed a smirk on her face and said, "Without the ability to agree or disagree. That is a humorous statement to me Dr. Chandler. I will address that momentarily. At any rate mother and daughter, as you put it, we will never be but within this 'truce' are you admitting you were wrong at Halcyon's wedding?"

Hannah became ashamed with Mudear at that very moment and things began to click in her head on how to get to the bottom of all of this.

McKenzie was about to explode but Presscott's soft spoken, but commanding voice calmed her down. "Mudear, Halcyon's wedding is not the issue at hand. Is this my way of apologizing for what happened between you and I at the wedding? I would have to honestly say absolutely not and under no circumstances am I apologizing for that. What I do apologize for is standing there and allowing the argument to take place the way it did. Never once did you take a moment to hear me out. Why are we not working on having a better mother/daughter relationship? And in addition to that, 'agree or disagree', the wedding is the most recent example of this statement. For Christ's sake you went all in over some borrowed lip gloss, really?" Presscott shocked everyone at the table, including herself, but she refused to allow Mudear to make her back down from this one.

Mudear leaned forward back to her perch on the edge of the overstuffed chair and simply said, "I do not want to have a mother/daughter relationship with you, that is my choice, I oppose greatly to the thought. Now I believe that we have nothing else to talk about, in fact, feel free to excuse yourself from the table." There was no expression in Mudear's voice or on her face as she raised her hand to Presscott to shoo her away from the table.

Hannah could no longer be quiet and in Presscott's defense she leaned forward to face Mudear with an absurd look on her face as she asked, "Do you really think that is necessary?"

McKenzie clutched both of her hands together tightly in her lap to keep herself from slapping the piss out of her mother.

Mudear never broke her gaze from Presscott's eyes as she answered Hannah, "It does not matter if it is necessary or not, I am tired of looking at her."

McKenzie could not take it anymore, she stood up with great force to reprimand Mudear but Presscott stopped her by saying, "Younger sister of mine, it's okay, this is my battle and I am now ready to fight."

Now Mudear and Presscott were in a staring match that they were both equally determined to win.

Mudear became amused with Presscott's determination and asked, "Was the purpose of that statement intended to scare me?"

With that question on the table unanswered, the wine orders were brought into the dining room and Hannah escorted the server to the door and explained that they would call when they were ready to order. In that time words were not passed between Mudear and Presscott.

Once Hannah was seated again Presscott answered Mudear with, "I have never said words to you with the hopes of them scaring you *Beth*." Presscott knew what buttons to push on Mudear and calling Mudear *Beth* was the ultimate disrespect. Presscott took another drink of her water and enjoyed a quiet delight in watching Mudear's amusing expression turn into furry.

When Presscott called Mudear *Beth* her two sisters immediately calmed down and cringed in their seats.

Mudear squinted her eyes at Presscott and the verbal battle began.

"Why would you disrespect me like that? I am your mother."

"But if given the choice, you would not be my mother. Why disrespect me by calling me daughter?"

"Obviously I did not have that choice so now what Presscott?"

"Since you are the mother why don't you tell me now what?"

"What do you want from me Presscott?"

"Let's start at the beginning, how did all of this start?"

"I don't think you can handle that."

"I think you should let me be the judge of that."

"Okay 'Miss Psychologist' I'll tell you."

Presscott was not prepared to hear what her mother had to say and she definitely did not approve of the circumstances that surrounded this conversation.

Then Mudear bluntly said, "I don't know if you are your father's child."

As oxymoronic as that statement was, it almost knocked Hannah and McKenzie out of their seats. The meaning of the statement pierced Presscott's heart as if it were an arrow set on fire.

In the spirit of keeping her stance strong Presscott asked, "So you treat me worse than a stepchild because of your personal indiscretions. I had nothing to do with that. "

Hannah went into attorney mode and pushed the record button on her mini tape recorder that permanently resided in her purse.

McKenzie at this point was crushed and she kept repeating, "Scottie you are my sister."

While Presscott reached over to comfort McKenzie, Mudear continued, "Presscott that sounded like an accusation to me. What are you accusing me of?"

That question was too easy for McKenzie not to

lash out and she stared straight into Mudear's eyes and said, "It sounds like to me that the great Elizabeth Ellington is a ho. Mommy you a ho?"

Presscott had to fight hard to get McKenzie's attention once she released her wrath on her favorite opponent, Mudear. "McKenzie Nicole Ellington you will not stoop to Mudear's level today. I can handle myself. Now you sit here quietly or you wait in another room."

Once the dining room got quiet and McKenzie composed herself, Presscott turned to Mudear giving her permission to respond to the accusation that stood like a white elephant in the middle of the table.

Mudear looked at Presscott with no emotion present and said, "I was raped during the same time that Stanley and I decided to have children. You were born exactly nine months after the rape and I have hated you ever since your conception."

As hurt as Presscott was she automatically went into Psychology mode as she tried to figure this all out. "Mudear how do you justify the means? Why are you okay with hating an innocent child that had nothing to do with a violent crime towards you? And we know for sure that the child is your flesh and blood."

Mudear was no longer on her perch and she seemed as if her heart wanted to reach out to Presscott but then she answered, "I did not then and still do not need to justify my actions, I just needed someone to blame and you were that someone."

"And I guess yo dumb ass didn't get a paternity test. Ooh I wish I was the one with no ties to you!" McKenzie was so angry.

With that statement Mudear stripped away everything that was foundational in her world and in her life. The only thing Presscott knew for sure was that Jonathan loved her and that was where she needed to be right now. Presscott swallowed hard and asked Mudear her last question, "Why do you still not know who my birth father is?"

With no emotion and staring Presscott right in her eyes, Mudear answered, "I did not then and still do not care to know. I have no love for you and I certainly do not care for you. My womb just happened to be the one to assist in your birth. There is nothing maternal for you in me. Being referred to as your mother is just a technicality." Even Mudear felt a little sting with her answer.

McKenzie and Hannah had reached their limit of being silent. While they were letting Mudear have it, Presscott sat back in her seat completely depleted. She then composed herself. Her head was spinning with unbelief and never ending questions. How could a mother break the maternal instinct code? Presscott thought it was innate; mothers are not allowed to hate their own children, right? Presscott began to understand why Mudear could never be her cynosure.

Mudear never took her eyes off of Presscott.

Then Presscott reached down and picked up her purse and stood up. She wanted to say something magical to Mudear to fix this but she had nothing so she just walked over to a chess board that was set up and laid the king and queen down on one side. Then she turned to Mudear with one lone tear making a path down her cheek and said in a whisper, "I will never fault you for the rape. The game is over. You win. Congratulations on your victory."

Mudear raised her wine glass to Presscott with a defiant smirk at the corner of her lips and nodded her head to accept her triumph.

Presscott left the dining room undetected by her sisters.

HOW TO CARRY ON

As far as Presscott was concerned she was a Chandler at heart and she wanted to be with Jonathan. While she drove up Peachtree Street she gained her composure and called the Ellington Hub. Thirty minutes later she was strapping herself into an overstuffed chair on an Ellington Lear Jet headed to Washington, D.C. It was a very short flight but it felt like a twenty-four flight to Presscott. Tears silently fell from her eyes for the duration of the flight because she could not believe how heartless her mother was to her. She knew Jonathan would not have answers for her but she needed him to just hold her. She wanted to be as close as she could to him; she needed to feel his calefaction.

As the plane descended into Washington, D.C she cleared her throat and called Jonathan to let him know that she would be at his hotel in about forty-five minutes. Jonathan, concerned with his wife's well-being, cancelled his meetings for the rest of the day and made his way to the hotel. Jonathan knew that Mudear would be written all over this problem.

It had started to drizzle while Jonathan waited outside the main entrance of the hotel for Presscott. Then a black town car pulled up, the back door opened with no assistance from the driver and Presscott stepped out. Jonathan watched her as she put on some Chloe shades to hide her tear stained eyes. She wore no jacket; she was only adorned in a velour jogging suit. The pants hugged her thighs and the sleeveless top exposed her mid drift, her tennis shoes were the exact same color as her jogging suit. Jonathan felt like the worst man in the world. His wife was drop dead gorgeous and he could not protect her from the person that hurt her the worse, her self-absorbed mother. Jonathan then walked over to the driver and tipped him generously with two fifty dollar bills. Presscott was so engrossed with her thoughts that she had not noticed Jonathan.

The rain was cold but the temperature did not register to her. When she finally caught sight of Jonathan the tears from her eyes begin to fall again. She dropped her head out of embarrassment because she now had to tell her husband that she might not be who she had led him to believe she was. How was he going to accept that fact, he may leave her? She always believed that he didn't care about the fame or fortune. Truth be told she would give up the money, fame, and recognition just to be with Jonathan. What was she going to do? Then she felt his hand gently usher her face up to face his.

He was wearing the boyish smile on his face that he wore after they made love.

She swallowed hard and bit her bottom lip.

He removed the shades from her face.

Her bottom lip eased slowly out of her teeth's grip.

The water from the rain matted her short haircut

to her head and her bangs stuck to her forehead right above her brow.

They were face to face and Presscott repeated in a whisper, "I'm sorry," through tears.

Jonathan's heart was breaking to see his wife like this. He held her face in his hands and he felt her try to look down, then she tried to look away. His hands kept her eyes trained on him.

She reached her right hand up to rest on his left shoulder and then she titled her head ever so slightly to the right and let out a soft deflated sigh.

"I love you Scottie," Jonathan repeated between soft kisses to her lips until she accepted the expression of his love to her with returned kisses.

Then she held him as close as she could to her body and then whispered, "I love you back," in his ear.

He let out a sigh and held her tighter.

Then she whispered in his ear again, "Honey I'm wet."

Jonathan was happy to hear her say that and he looked down at her mischievously.

She smiled back at him and said, "Honey it's raining."

Jonathan flashed that boyish smile as he realized that it was raining and Presscott was drenched. He then escorted her quickly into the lobby of the hotel by her hand.

Presscott was literally trying to shake the events of the day from her head and just enjoy being with Jonathan but it was too much for her. As they rode the elevator up to the Penthouse Suite the tears began to fall again. Jonathan just stood on the opposite side of the elevator and watched her.

When they got off of the elevator he went into the bathroom and programmed the tub for a hot bubble bath. He grabbed a robe off of the back of the door, laid it out neatly on the bed and walked over to Presscott. She was standing by the window watching the city buzz below her, wiping tears from her eyes. Jonathan gently took her hand and walked her to the center of the floor. He began to undress her starting with her top.

She stood with her head bowed. She was shivering cold and the tears never stopped falling.

When she was completely undressed he picked her up and laid her on top of the robe on the bed. He carefully placed her arms in the sleeves then seated himself in the chair across from her and she rolled over to the edge of the bed to face Jonathan.

"Mudear told me today that Stanley Preston Ellington may not be my father and that's why she hates me." Presscott said those words through a voice full of confusion.

Jonathan listened to everything Presscott had to say as she regurgitated the day's events with no interruptions and when she was done he simply said, "You are a Chandler. You are the best thing that ever happened to me and my family."

She knew he was right but she had to ask, "If I am stripped from all of the Ellington privileges are you going to leave me?" She couldn't believe those words came out of her mouth; she had never been given any reason to believe that Jonathan didn't love her for her.

Jonathan was hurt and angered by the question but he knew his words could not reflect those emotions. Not now.

So he simply said, "I never fell in love with the Ellington privileges, I fell in love with you. Honey I'm not going anywhere and your sisters aren't going anywhere either."

Then she immediately began to apologize for the question and explained how the turn of the day's events were making her question everything that she thought she knew.

"Honey," Jonathan began his response, "I understand why that question has to exist, why it has to be asked, and why it has to be answered honestly. You are going to question everything and some things you will question multiple times, even about me. I vow to answer every question honestly as many times as you ask. We are going to get through this.

Presscott stared at the floor as she began to process things in her head, and then she asked with a straight face as she looked into his eyes, "When you decided to propose to me, was it before or after you found out I was an Ellington?

Jonathan didn't know that the inquisition was going to start immediately but he answered honestly. He had just vowed to her that he would. "I always knew who you were. My heart was groomed just for you. I proposed to you because I was finally able to throw caution to the wind."

"Really?"

"Girl you are still the finest thing going anywhere."

Presscott had two more questions to ask him but she decided to hold off because she realized that every answer that he gave her would only lead to another question and she didn't want to waste the warmth of the bubble bath.

As Presscott walked into the bathroom, Jonathan said, "The proposal had nothing to do with Stanley and company. You expressed genuine love for me and did I mention how fine you are?"

That's what Jonathan was after, that genuine smile she just flashed him.

She turned to Jonathan and beckoned him to come to her with her index finger. When he got into arm's reach of her, she began removing his tie and said, "My turn now."

five:

THE MORNING AFTER THE BRUNCH

McKenzie woke up the next morning and everything that Mudear put them through the previous day flooded her mind. As she reviewed the day's events she felt sick to her stomach. Then she wondered what other family secrets she and her sisters had yet to uncover. *After all we are the untouchable Ellington's*, McKenzie said out loud to herself.

McKenzie's thoughts were interrupted by the sudden realization that Presscott was in D.C. with Jonathan for the next few days and she had the Chandler Mansion to herself. McKenzie jumped out of bed, brushed her teeth and washed her face. She put on a new sports bra with matching yoga pants. She accessorized the outfit with a matching banana clip and jazz shoes. She gave herself one last look in the full length mirror in the bathroom to check the gauge on her "cute meter." As she was pleased with the reading, she grabbed her water bottle and made her way to the dance studio. She made an extra stop by the kitchen and requested that a charbroiled chicken salad with no tomatoes be served to her for lunch in three hours on the patio outside of the dance studio. As she began to walk away she remembered something so she turned with a flirtatious smile.

"Marty," she began her request, "will you make me some sweet Georgia moonshine to go with my salad?"

Marty loved whenever McKenzie flirted with him and he answered through a blush, "Madam Kennie, I will do anything for you."

That made McKenzie's day; she loved the way he made sweet tea and she would only drink his. "Thank you," she replied as she kissed him on the cheek.

When McKenzie walked into the dance studio, she closed the door softly as if not to disturb a sleeping infant. She looked around admiring all of the carvings, paintings, and the well-polished cherry wood floor begging for a pair of feet to grace its surface with a massage. McKenzie glided to the center of the floor, and stretched in reverence to the art and spirit of the dance. She then made her way over to the stereo and pushed the play button for the C.D. player. The words from Kelly Price's sophomore album filled the studio, "I didn't call you in the midnight hour, I wouldn't tuck you in and turn the night light out..."

McKenzie forced air out of her stomach in the form of a laugh and programmed the song to repeat and began to warm up. Her thoughts drifted to Michael, she thought of all the good times and the bad times. She was happy, she was sad, she was furious, she was at peace, she was confused and uncertain all at the same time. What, when, and how was she going to deal with all of this? Will this ever make sense to her? If she ever had children, how was she going to explain this period of her life to them? Will she ever understand all of this herself?

While she danced she changed the words mentally to the song to fit her particular situation. By the time McKenzie pulled herself out of her thoughts she was drenched with sweat, out of breath and answered some of the questions that she had tried desperately to ignore. She decided not to sell her studio and loft in New York. She also allowed herself to experience closure with the baby spiritually and emotionally. Well she closed the book on this part of life so she thought.

Then she walked over to the C.D. player and programmed it for random play. OutKast, "Bombs Over Baghdad," filled the room and she bobbed her head with a smirk on her face. When the song ended McKenzie had to dance to it again because there was a freedom that she had never experienced before and she needed to saturate herself in it. Presscott had a great love for music and it showed as the C.D. player switched from disc to disc. McKenzie had every style of dance running through her veins and it showed in everything she did and every word she spoke. Then Karen Clark Sheard's "Just For Me," came on and that was when the healing within her heart began. She started with Russian Ballet and mixed it with Expressive Praise dance. Something was happening in her heart, her mind, and her soul. What was going on inside? She ran toward the patio door on her tiptoes leading with her chest then made a mental note that her lunch was being served.

Marty stood right inside of the door in utter amazement of what he saw and heard and without realizing it, he was beginning to get a little choked up. By the time the song ended McKenzie was sobbing her repentance unto the Lord face down in the middle of the floor as Marty did the same, silently leaving the studio.

McKenzie tried to get up several times but every time she tried to move she felt like she weighed a ton. She finally stopped trying to get up and just laid down on her back and let it all go for about fifteen minutes. Then Erik Satie, Gymnopedie #1, cleansing and pure. McKenzie was very familiar with the piece, but she had only heard the piano and guitar version of the song, but this was a full orchestra playing. Now she knew things would be okay.

When she got up she headed straight to the shower in the studio and programmed it for an intense massage and had the center floor raised to four feet. After her shower she felt cleansed inside and out. Afterwards she enjoyed her lunch as she listened to Gymnopedie again and the tea was perfect.

While McKenzie ate her lunch she called her Realtor, Lance, in New York.

The phone rang, "Lance speaking," the voice answered very calmly.

"Hey Lance, it's your favorite Ellington," McKenzie said in a peace offering kind of way.

"Everybody knows Presscott is my favorite Ellington, now who is this playing on my phone?" Lance was getting irritated.

"McKenzie," she said through a big smile.

"Oh, the family fool," he was very annoyed with her. "I haven't put your properties on the market yet. And what's this I hear about you shooting up your own shit? Just because you are an Ellington and Mr. Obama is president doesn't mean you can cut the fool whenever you want. You need to realize those are two very heavy reasons for you to stop all of this nonsense. For some reason God chose to bless you, the fool, better than most and you can't seem to get it together. What is your problem?" Lance was the only person outside of her sisters that she cared about being in right standing with.

She needed to get back in right standing with Lance.

"I apologize and you are right. I am use to doing whatever I want, when I want and never having to deal with consequences. Presscott has always made sure everything was okay for all of us."

Lance asked, "And who covers Presscott?"

That question lingered as a dagger in McKenzie's heart. She shook her head as she tried to get back on task with Lance then she asked, "Why were the properties not put on the market?"

"Because I took a gander and guessed that these were very impulsive decisions that you made because you think you saw your man having sex with your protégé." Lance was going to tell her exactly what she needed to know.

McKenzie was starting to feel sick to her stomach then she closed her eyes and asked in a mono tone voice, "Please tell me what all you know?"

She heard Lance excuse himself. Then he said, "Nicole the tattoos gave it away. When I looked at the tape, the guy had a tattoo on his neck and the girl had a tattoo on the front of her foot."

"How did you see the tape?" She asked the question still whispering with her eyes still closed massaging her temples.

"Your muscle wanted me to find the girl."

"And did you?"

"Yes."

"Who is she?"

"Some girl strung out on a narcotic that got paid five thousand dollars to sleep with some random dude in the Ellington dance studio."

"Is she okay?"

"Sammy put her in a rehab and the last time I checked she wasn't doing so well."

"What about the guy?"

"I can't find him. I think he got the money and left."

The phone line became loudly silent.

Then Lance said, "Don't worry Nicole, we'll get to the bottom of this."

Things were not adding up in her head. She could not think of any one that would want to sabotage her and Michael's relationship. Also, her and Michael talked about marriage and parenthood together, what's really wrong here she wondered to herself.

McKenzie let out a deep breath and said, "Thank you Lance for everything." She stopped talking for a brief moment to gather rational thoughts then she asked, "Can I fly you to Atlanta? I would like to induct you as my voice of reason. Is that okay?"

"Only if you promise not to put me up at your momma's estate."

"Done."

"Done? That was too easy. Where am I staying?"

"With your favorite Ellington."

"Nicole don't play with my emotions, I'm starting to kinda like you again. Where?"

"With me at Presscott's."

"Okay, realistically I can leave New York in two days."

"Lance you have to sign a confidentially contract."

"Okay."

TEXT MESSAGE:

Hi ladies bck 2morrow @ 4 rr mtng @ 545 love u guys Scottie.

six:

Presscott returned to Atlanta as scheduled and her Escalade and a town car were waiting while the plane taxied into the Ellington hub. As usual, the town car was for the luggage that was to return to the Chandler Mansion.

Presscott then made her way to Flowers Road and parked at the railroad tracks. Presscott took a moment to take a deep breath and call Jonathan to let him know that she had arrived safely.

While leaving a message on Jonathan's phone she saw a platinum Jaguar come speeding around the corner. Once it was up on the gravel, it fish tailed and drifted to an abrupt stop. When the debris settled around the car, the door on the driver side opened slowly. Before the driver could get out of the Jaguar, a 1974 cream colored convertible Super Bug pulled right in front of the Jaguar. The top was down on the Super Bug. Presscott emerged from her black Escalade putting her Chloe shades atop her head. She walked towards the Super Bug swinging her arm back to close the truck's door smiling at Hannah still seated. Then Presscott said, "No one else can make this simply ugly car look as good like you."

Hannah was thrilled to hear her sister's voice.

Presscott sounded like her old self and Hannah just wanted to apologize for everything that Mudear ever did to her that was wrong. Hannah was overcome with emotion by the sight of her oldest sister that a tear or two escaped from her eyes.

Presscott reached into her pocket and pulled out a tissue, opened the driver's door and wiped her sister's eyes. "Hannah, it's okay, I'm okay, and all of us will eventually be okay."

These were the words that Presscott whispered to her sister in an attempt to comfort and console her. Presscott then grabbed Hannah's hand and led her to the Jaguar.

McKenzie stepped out of the Jaguar just before her sisters reached her and they all stood for a brief moment looking one another over and then the three embraced.

RAILROAD MEETINGS

Railroad Meetings were created when Presscott was twelve years old. Presscott got a ninety-eight on a Social Studies report and she was ecstatic. She did all the research on her own. All of her charts and pictures she created herself and she proofed her own report, word for word. Mudear was the only one at home when Presscott got home and she wanted to share her success with her mother first, hoping that her grade could possibly be used as a bargaining chip for a little acceptance. Presscott controlled her excitement as she explained her project to her mother, and Mudear's response was, "When will you ever learn that I don't like you and that your successes great or small mean nothing to me?"

Presscott felt her little face get warm and her eyes began to burn as her focus blurred by the tears forming in her eyes. The knot in her throat was so strong that it would not allow her to release a sound but the tears would not stop streaming down her face. When McKenzie got home from school with Hannah and Halcyon in tow, they found Presscott standing in the spot Mudear left her in silently crying; at least thirty minutes had lapsed. McKenzie dropped her books on the floor and ran to Presscott and tried to get her to explain what happened to her. When McKenzie realized that Presscott was not going to talk, she emphatically yelled for Mudear to come quickly. Mudear got to the room as quick as she could and out of breath and with much concern she inquired about what the problem could possibly be. McKenzie pointed to Presscott and with fear in her voice she said, "Do something, look at Scottie she won't talk and...."

Mudear cut McKenzie words off and asked very sternly, "You called me in here for this?" And when she said the word *this* she pointed towards Presscott and had a scowl on her face as she looked at McKenzie.

"Something is wrong, Mudear please," and in the middle of McKenzie's pleading for help Mudear walked out of the room throwing her hands up in aggravation.

In that very moment McKenzie had so much hatred for Mudear that she actually felt herself age. With every ounce of hatred McKenzie was experiencing she marched to the hallway entrance and said, "Oh *Beth*," McKenzie's voice had turned evil, "you are a bitch." McKenzie now had everyone's attention including Presscott's.

Mudear returned to the room the girls were in with a belt and beat Presscott abusively until McKenzie apologized for calling her *Beth*.

Dinner was in silence except for Hannah and Halcyon trying to decide how to smile for their school pictures. Presscott asked to be excused without taking one bite of food but she was excused, with McKenzie following soon after.

Presscott packed up a small bag which included her books and a flashlight while McKenzie watched. McKenzie asked Presscott question after question, in which Presscott answered not one. Then Presscott said without looking at McKenzie, "If you are coming with me make sure you get your homework, a flashlight, something to snack on and put on some warmer clothes. I am leaving in ten minutes."

McKenzie, in silence, did exactly what Presscott said and their journey led them to the railroad tracks on Flowers Road. This soon became the only place where Presscott felt comfortable to dream, to smile, to feel proud and to be happy. The other Ellington girls did not adopt the railroad tracks as their personal haven of safety but they understood what it meant to Presscott and they each secretly vowed to protect it for her.

seven:

Stanley Preston Ellington was the man that headed the Ellington family passively. He married Elizabeth Wells against her own free will. Stanley was sympathetic to her feelings about the arranged marriage but he dared not to go against his father's wishes. The marriage union of the Ellingtons and the Wells was nothing short of "The Miracle" of all ages. The union of the two families was something that had been desired for generations and it would make the two families the wealthiest family that had ever existed in time.

Stanley Ellington worked very obediently for his father and Mr. Wells, Mudear's father, until they both died. The only thing that Stanley showed respect for was the family crest that joined the two families together. Elizabeth did not love Stanley, but he had fallen for her while they were still in high school. When both fathers had passed on, Stanley went to Elizabeth and told her that they needed to marry for status purposes only and when she was ready to divorce him all she had to do was let him know and he'd take care of everything. Her every wish would still be his command. With time she fell in love with Stanley as well but she was so accustomed to making him pay for her unwanted marriage to him that she did not know how to treat him otherwise.

When Stanley and Elizabeth were introduced to one another as future husband and wife; they were in their senior year of high school. They both attended the same boarding school in Nantucket. Stanley always admired Elizabeth from a distance and wished on every star he saw that he could be Dexter Jenkins.

Dexter Jenkins was well built, a great basketball player, he would be the class valedictorian and held the heart of Elizabeth Wells. In fact every guy that attended that school wished they were Dexter Jenkins because of Elizabeth Wells.

Elizabeth was so well put together, in spite of the tragedy that she had to weather in the public's eye. Elizabeth was extensively interviewed every three years about how she was doing without the guide of her loving mother. She always held her head high, she was always polite and she had to be the sweetest Georgia Peach that God had ever created.

Now she was being told that she would have to marry three months after her graduation and her suitor's name was not Dexter Jenkins. That was the thing that finally made the great Elizabeth Wells crack. On the outside, her smile remained and she appeared to be the perfect fiancé, according to the media. She played up the absent love affair for the media and family but Stanley knew differently. Whenever he took her out on dates she would sometimes have Dexter meet them at their destination. She would disappear with Dexter for hours and often returned home without Stanley.

The only person that knew what pain and anguish Elizabeth was going through was her Nanny, Miss Sue. Miss Sue often had long talks with Mr. Wells to see if he would at least talk to his daughter to find out if she wanted to marry Stanley. Mr. Wells was not having it, this union was "The Miracle" of all ages and he was going to make sure that it happened no matter what.

Once the wedding had taken place and Stanley and Elizabeth were on their way to Aruba for their honeymoon, she informed him that Dexter was on his family vacation in Aruba. She also informed Stanley that she planned on spending as much time with Dexter as she could. That led to their first and only argument as a married couple in which her resentment for Stanley reached an all-time high. When they landed in Aruba they did not speak to one another. After they were settled in their suite, they were informed that Mr. Dexter Jenkins was there to see them. Stanley was furious and through clenched teeth demanded that Dexter be shown in. For the first time with Stanley, Elizabeth felt uneasy where Dexter was concerned.

Dexter entered the suite and he was not his usual upbeat self. He walked over to shake Stanley's hand with congratulations on the marriage and to apologize for his absence. Then he asked Stanley, "May I speak with you and your bride please?"

Stanley looked puzzled as he looked over at Elizabeth. Before Stanley could answer, Elizabeth answered yes for him. Dexter out of respect for the marriage asked Stanley again if he could speak to both of them. Stanley with a puzzled look still residing on his face with furrowed brow nodded his head positively. The three of them then walked into the lounge area of the suite and Dexter broke things off with Elizabeth, apologized to Stanley for his actions over the summer, explained why he kept the relationship going with the great Elizabeth Wells, and assured Stanley that he and Elizabeth had never been intimate together.

Elizabeth sat in silence, body temperature rising with her fist clenched and arms hugging her waist. Dexter with a soft voice apologized for hurting Elizabeth. They all froze in that moment in time because they realized that they were truly not "lucky" because they were born with silver spoons in their mouths. They all wondered if they would ever be able to or allow their children to make their own decisions in life. They all recognized one another's pain in the whole messed up scenario of what had just taken place and was to come.

In that realization, Stanley spoke, "I know that you truly and honestly love Dexter. I have never had the opportunity to love you; I have only admired what I thought I knew of you in school. I have envied Dexter because he was with the great Elizabeth Wells. I did not know that you and I had been chosen to marry. If I would have known that I would have told the both of you and we could have figured something out. But it is now a reality and what has happened, happened and this is what I propose to the both of you. You two may continue your relationship and I will not disturb that. Elizabeth, you and I will not be intimate. In the event that Elizabeth becomes pregnant by you Dexter, I will give the child my name to maintain the front. I will not get in the way of you and your children. I cannot admit that I am in love with Elizabeth, but I know love when I see it and Elizabeth loves you. I do not want to and cannot compete with that. The only thing that I ask is that the two of you keep the lines of communications open with me so we will always have our stories straight." With that said, he left so discreetly that no one, not even Dexter and Elizabeth, realized that he had actually left the room.

Within three months Dexter and Elizabeth dwindled into nothing because Stanley made it okay and too easy for them to be together. Dexter thought he had a pretty good deal going; his girlfriend's husband excused him of any responsibilities if a baby happened to come along. Elizabeth, on the other hand, weighed the cost of everything and she could not justify being intimate with anyone else other than her husband. Dexter, tired of her unwillingness to have sex with him, so he called her on the telephone one day and simply said, "We're done." He did not offer an explanation and she was relieved.

Elizabeth immediately began to put all of her energy into finding out who her husband was. He had intrigued her with the way he spoke and she wanted to know about his travels abroad. She wanted to know why he feared his father the way he did and why his mother never had her own ideas about anything.

One night at the dinner table Elizabeth asked Stanley if they could move into the same bedroom. He hesitated and then said yes. He wanted to know desperately what happened between Elizabeth and Dexter but he dare not ask; if and when she wanted him to know she would tell. One year had passed since Elizabeth and Stanley were married and they had not been intimate with one another. He never cheated on her and neither did she on him after Dexter. They fell in love with one another within that year but most importantly they developed an amazing friendship and respect towards each other. The first time they made love there was a fourth of July celebration that happened just for them in their bedroom. Neither one of them left the bedroom for three days. Elizabeth was too embarrassed to allow the outside world see her because of what she had experienced for the first time. Stanley was just happy. The Ellingtons were finally becoming a family the right way.

One day Elizabeth was out shopping at her favorite Gucci Shop in Phipps Plaza. While she was checking out the wallets she saw a familiar face looking at her from the display window. She finished her transaction and walked out of the store with a puzzled look on her face. She looked right first, no familiar faces. She looked left and there standing in front of her was Dexter Edward Jenkins. He still looked good; actually he looked better than he ever did in high school. Dexter reached out to hug Elizabeth but she took a step back and offered her hand instead.

"Wow...it's chilly in here." Dexter said sarcastically.

The corner of Elizabeth's mouth displayed a smirk and

then she said with much confidence, "How are you doing Mr. Jenkins and what brings you to town?"

Dexter could not believe the cold reception from the great Elizabeth Wells Ellington. "Umph... I never thought it would come to this Beth." Dexter said with disbelief.

With no emotion Elizabeth said, "Well it has, what are you doing in town?"

Dexter shook his head in an attempt to bring himself back to the present moment. "I have moved to Atlanta because I bought the Atlanta Hawks and I wanted to see if I could re-establish a love affair that I once had."

Still showing no emotion or concern for what Dexter had just said, Elizabeth responded with, "Congratulations and good luck with all of your future endeavors."

Elizabeth began to walk off and Dexter asked behind her, "Do you love him Beth?"

Without a thought Elizabeth turned towards Dexter with about five steps between them and said, "Yes I love him."

Dexter then closed the gap between the two of them and asked breathlessly, "Do you still love me?"

Elizabeth was absolutely amazed and simply answered, "No." She then turned and walked away from him.

While she was in rout to the Ellington Estate she

chose to stop by Stanley's office to tell him what had just happened. When Elizabeth saw Stanley she became emotional. She could not explain her emotions but they were present and she kept realizing just how much she loved Stanley. She felt like a jerk for treating him the way she had for so long and she thanked God that all of that was over.

Two weeks had passed since Elizabeth's run in with Dexter, and if the truth were told she was done with it after she told Stanley what happened. Stanley had to be overseas for the next six to eight weeks to open a new company. Whenever this happened Elizabeth joined Stanley after the first two weeks. This time she would not make it to Stanley's side in two weeks. As usual, Elizabeth would go to the airport with her husband and cry as she watched his plane leave the ground.

She requested that her Bentley be brought to the airport because she wanted to drive herself home. It was raining and her security followed closely behind. As she went through the intersection of Peachtree and Lenox, a car ran the red light and hit the security car that was following her. In all of her security briefings in the past she was taught in the event of a car accident, if she was safe, never to the leave the car. She was to first make sure that all the doors were locked and then call the local police.

Elizabeth's thoughts were on the plane with Stanley and without thinking she drove her car to the side of the road and jumped out of her car. Her security guards were like brothers to her and she needed to make sure they were okay. While Elizabeth ran to the corner in her high-heeled Burberry boots, she did not realize with the rain falling in her eyes that an unmarked black van was driving towards her with the side sliding door open. A set of muscular arms grabbed her around her waist and ushered her onto the moving van's floor.

Never once did she scream. She began to concentrate on the movements and turns of the van. She heard a deep male voice say over a walkie-talkie, "No resistance... yes sir Mr. Jenkins..."

Elizabeth's thoughts were frantically searching for answers and a solution and an escape route but she lay in the floor of the van as if she were dead. After about twenty minutes the van stopped. She heard the driver's window being rolled down. She heard five numbers being put into a keypad or was it four numbers and a # key or an * key being pushed at the end. She heard what sounded like a heavy gate open to her right. Then the van drove up a slight incline and then bared around to the left. She assumed the van was driving around to the back of a building of some sort. Then the van made a slow tight right and stopped. She had not moved since she had been in the van. The ignition was turned off and all of the doors were opened at once.

Elizabeth was pulled to the edge of the of the van's floor and in one motion she was hoisted over a strong shoulder like a sack of potatoes. She opened her eyes to try and assess her surroundings but it was too dark for her eyes to adjust. Then as she was carried through the threshold of the first doorway she finally made out that she was at a house from a light that was on over a stove. The man that was carrying her walked to the refrigerator and got something to drink. While he was drinking, he stood in the middle of the kitchen floor with his back to a counter that had unopened mail on it. Elizabeth saw the name *Dexter Jenkins* on the mail and then memorized the address. She knew automatically that this was not about money, it was personal. But why?

At about that time the pressure from the blood rushing to her head ushered a massive headache and she did not know how much longer she could play dead hanging over this man's shoulder. The man then threw something in the trash and then walked up a short flight of stairs. He walked to the end of a hallway and walked through a door on the right. He gently laid her on what felt like a mattress with no sheets. The man straightened out her clothes and said, "I'm sorry Mrs. Ellington, I wish I ain't got nerve ta do dis but I gotta. By da way I know you up... an fo da record you are pur-dee."

Elizabeth could not figure out what was going to happen next but she decided to accept her kidnapper's apology and she whispered without moving her lips, "Thank you."

He smiled, looked her over one more time and left the room.

To Elizabeth it felt like an eternity had passed but only a few short minutes had passed and she heard the door open again and prayed that it was her kidnapper but it was Dexter. She heard him playfully call her *Beth* and she decided right then that she hated the name *Beth* and she would no longer answer to it. He walked over to the bed and rubbed the side of her face with the back of his hand.

She did not move.

He kissed her softly on her lips.

She did not move.

He softly kissed the tip of her nose.

She did not move.

He then took the tip of his tongue and ran it up the

bridge of her nose.

She did not move.

He stopped in the center of her forehead and kissed her.

She opened her eyes immediately and with her right hand dug her fingernails into his Adams apple.

He could not yell out for help. She maneuvered herself on top of him and looked in his eyes and asked, "What do you want with me?" Her words were full of hate as she spat the question through clenched teeth. Elizabeth thought she had the upper hand on Dexter but he overpowered her little body. She fought him with everything she had to no avail.

Dexter raped her several times through the night. He never used a condom. He went down on her and caused her to reach an ecstasy that she never knew existed. Through tears of pleasure and pain she apologized to Stanley verbally. Every time Dexter penetrated her she had an orgasm. One day he tied her against the foot of the bed completely naked and performed anal sex on her. The discomfort caused her to yell in pain but by the time it was over she had reached yet another orgasm. Dexter held her captive for a week and continuously raped her. Then he offered her to her kidnappers by announcing loudly, "Beth is primed and ready if you want her. You know what to do with her when you're done."

The kidnapper that apologized to her entered the room forty five minutes later with a fleece blanket and found her balled up in a corner naked. He was the only one at the house. He walked over to her and stooped down in front of her with the blanket resting over one knee. "Mrs. Ellington." He whispered her name.

It sounded like the nice kidnapper to her but something was different about his voice.

"I'm going to take you home." It was the nice kidnapper's voice but the voice was southern and educated; no slang apparent at all.

She finally looked up into his face to see if he was telling the truth and he smiled a warm smile; the tears without cue began to fall with no sound. He wrapped her in the blanket, gathered all her clothes and carried her outside.

She noticed that it was dark out.

He very carefully placed her in the passenger seat and reclined the seat all the way back. He got in on the driver side of his car and drove straight to the Ellington Estate.

Right before they reached the Ellington Estate, the nice kidnapper pulled over to the side of the road. He then reached into the glove box and pulled out a small handgun. He made sure that it was loaded and the safety was off. Elizabeth just watched him quietly and decided to herself that she had no more fight and no more tears. The nice kidnapper reassured Elizabeth that the gun was just his way of securing a safe entrance onto the Estate. Then they drove to the security house at the front gate. A security guard stepped out of the guardhouse and greeted the driver with courtesy. The nice kidnapper rolled down the driver's window and the security guard said, "Good evening Sir. The Ellington's are not accepting any visitors tonight and since you are not immediate family I cannot grant you access to the grounds."

The nice kidnapper smiled at the guard and said, "I understand but I have something that Mr. Ellington really wants."

The guard was starting to get annoyed and he let out a little sigh and said, "Sir please feel free to leave a note and your package here and I will deliver it to Mr. Ellington myself." The security guard motioned to a second security guard for back up purposes.

All of the Ellington staff at the house were unsettled from the first time that they were briefed on Mrs. Ellington's disappearance.

"I understand Officer," the kidnapper began, "but I have Mrs. Ellington in my passenger seat and I need to take her to Mr. Ellington." He was very calm and persistent.

The two security guards looked at each other and drew their guns from their holsters. The second guard moved around the front of the car watching the nice kidnapper searching for some truth in his expression. When he got to the passenger side of the car he commanded the kidnapper to move the blanket off of her face. The nice kidnapper simply said, "Mrs. Ellington move the blanket from your face slowly because I have the gun pointed at your temple."

She did as the kidnapper said and she looked out of the passenger window and she saw Reggie looking down at her. She asked the kidnapper if she could roll down her window and he said, "Yes ma'am."

She rolled her window down and assured Reggie that she was okay; then she instructed him to do exactly what the kidnapper said. Both security guards agreed and placed their guns back in their holsters.

The kidnapper began to give directions, "First call the authorities and the ambulance. Then call Mr. Ellington and let him know that I am bringing Mrs. Ellington to the front door of the main house. Let him know that I will carry her into the house and put her wherever he wants me to. Instruct him not kiss her or remove the blanket. I will explain why when I get to him. Now lock down the front gate and escort me to the house. Also gentlemen, Mrs. Ellington is going to be fine because I can see in yall's eyes how much yall love her." With that the kidnapper took the bullets out of his gun and handed the bullets and the gun to Elizabeth.

The two security guards did exactly as the kidnapper instructed them to do and when they reached the front door of the main house Mr. Ellington was pacing in front of the door in his pajamas.

Mr. Ellington had a number of emotions flowing through him all at one time. When he assessed the situation for himself he let out a loud sigh of relief. Mr. Ellington tried to kiss Mrs. Ellington and the kidnapper stopped him gently. "Why!?!? Damn it! Why can I not kiss my own wife?" Mr. Ellington was emotionally spent and he needed the warmth of his wife as close to him as possible.

The kidnapper started his explanation with an apology and when he was done Mr. Ellington punched him square across the jaw. The kidnapper lost his balance but he did not retaliate because he understood where Mr. Ellington's anger was coming from. Mr. Ellington had absorbed what had happened to his wife and to his own surprise he jabbed left and upper cut right into the kidnapper's face.

The man stumbled and decided to defend himself. Mr. Ellington picked up the shovel for the fireplace and repeatedly hit the kidnapper in his left rib cage. Mr. Ellington did not stop swinging until he heard the nice kidnapper's ribs break. As he was falling to the living room floor Mr. Ellington reared his right foot back and caught the left side of the kidnapper's face with every ounce of disgust in his body and broke his jaw. Mr. Ellington was upset, with himself, and decided he would not be satisfied until all parties involved were dead. Then he whispered, "This was not part of the plan."

A month had passed since the kidnapping and rape and the Ellingtons were trying to piece their lives back together. They had to bury the two security guards that were following Mrs. Ellington that night. Elizabeth would not drive her car alone any more. Stanley no longer flew anywhere without her. Elizabeth was no longer left alone. One night Elizabeth woke up in the middle of the night throwing up. The Ellingtons wrote it off as her having a reaction to the nightmares she was still having from the rape. She would always tell Stanley exactly what the dreams were about, at least everything she could remember. They would then walk through the entire mansion to assure her that Dexter was not in the house. He would then rock her back to sleep.

This particular night Elizabeth violently awoke screaming "no" at the top of her lungs. Stanley was terrified by the sound and he immediately started to check to see if she was physically hurt. The cry came from somewhere deep within her; to Stanley she sounded like a wounded animal. This time she did not want to walk through the estate, she just wanted Stanley to hold her and he did.

Then she said, "I dreamed that our first baby was Dexter's child."

Stanley held Elizabeth tight as he felt every muscle tense up in his body. That was a haunting thought to Stanley's heart. Although, if that were true and the first born was a male child then maybe his plan would work.

Nine months later, the Ellington daughter, Presscott Elizabeth was born to Stanley Preston and Elizabeth Ellington. Presscott Elizabeth Ellington became the wealthiest African American heiress in the United States of America just because she was born.

eight:

Presscott and McKenzie followed each other to the Chandler mansion after the railroad meeting. McKenzie was extremely concerned about her older sister. She wondered how long it would be before the strong Presscott Elizabeth Chandler broke down. McKenzie also wondered if she would be able to handle it if her sister broke down while she was with her. She decided to talk to Presscott about her concerns when they got to the mansion.

When they settled in Presscott asked McKenzie if she wanted to meet for a nightcap in the Ellington Sista Lounge on the second floor. McKenzie agreed and they were both in the lounge five minutes later. Once they were both sipping on some white wine they sat on one of the overstuffed couches facing one another and McKenzie began with, "So big sister of mine... did you and Jonathan have great comfort sex or what?"

Presscott just looked at her sister and shook her head in mock disbelief. Presscott really wanted to make sure that her younger sister was okay because of the information that was shared about her conception and the abortion. How would this affect all of the Ellington daughters?

"Well I guess Mudear's bomb shell didn't affect you at all," Presscott said as she took another sip of wine.

"Scottie, Scottie, Scottie," McKenzie started in, "Now you know it affected me but what's more important? Tell me about the comfort sex."

Presscott laughed and then she said, "As always I will not give you the hot, heavy, sensual, earth quaking, toe curling, body quivering orgasmic details but I will tell you this..." Presscott had McKenzie's undivided attention, "We kissed in the rain, he undressed me and he gave me a bubble bath."

McKenzie said mischievously, "He did more than that because yo ass been glowing since I first saw you at the railroad tracks."

Presscott thought for a moment and then said, "I don't think I'm glowing Kennie, I just needed a well-deserved break and I am well rested right now." Presscott said it as serious as she could without smiling.

"Look atcha... well rested my ass... yeah he slapped that mojo on you."

Presscott had to admit that there was something different about the way they made love after the comfort sex. It became precious and sacred. "Oh my God," Presscott said underneath her breath.

McKenzie watched Presscott for a short moment as

she searched her memory for something. Then McKenzie started singing, "I'm gonna be an auntie, I'm gonna be an auntie."

Presscott looked at McKenzie with disbelief in her eyes. Could she have conceived during the comfort sex sessions that must have lasted and lasted.

"Scottie, if you are pregnant, I will buy a condo in Buckhead and move back to Atlanta permanently."

"Would you really?'

"I sure would, in a heart-beat."

"But I don't know if I am pregnant for real."

"Who cares, I need a condo in Buckhead anyway"

"No you don't, that's wasteful."

"I want my own place to live in while I'm in Atlanta."

"You have a furnished mansion on the estate."

"That I will never live in, now that's wasteful."

"But those were the first gifts that our parents gave to us."

McKenzie looked at her sister trying to figure out how to convey her present thoughts without hurting her and then Hannah walked through the door, "Hello again ladies, what is the topic of conversation on the table?" she asked as she got a bottle of water out of the refrigerator.

McKenzie said to Hannah in a very serious educated

voice, "I am trying to get our eldest sister to realize that all of the sex that she had over the past few days is going to grant us our 'Auntie Cards.'"

"Oh Scottie..."

Hannah's sincerity was cut off by Presscott's realistic truths, "Don't 'Oh Scottie' me. Here's the truth. I spent the three previous days with my husband. Yes we made love and it was, well I can't tell you what it was because those sort of adjectives have not yet been created, but we made love and boy did we make love and.... Well I am not pregnant."

Hannah sat on the coffee table facing her sisters and looked at Presscott for a brief moment then she said in a mock sermon, "Kennie."

McKenzie responded with, "Yes Sister Hannah."

Hannah continued with her sermon, "You know I am a friend of God's and therefore He tells me things about my precious loved ones."

McKenzie grabbed a tissue from the tissue box and fanned at Hannah encouraging her to, "Preach, preacha."

Hannah furrowed her brow, cleared her throat and said, "Now a woman has two different kinds of glows. One glow appears because she has made love for the first time. That's not the glow that young Scottie has. Young Scottie has the second kind of glow, which is the glow of conception. Do you see the glow Sister Kennie?"

"I see the glow, amen." McKenzie shouted and started singing *Jesus Loves the Little Children.* All three of them began to laugh at Hannah's sermon and McKenzie's singing, but they all had a since of urgency to resolve some bigger issues.

"Well sisters, 1 and 2." Hannah started with a more serious tone and all of the laughing ceased. "I am no longer staying at the Ellington Estate," she announced.

Presscott and McKenzie looked at each other with confused expressions.

"Where are you staying Han?" Presscott inquired.

"I will be staying at the Ritz Carlton downtown until the Johnson Mansion is ready for me." Hannah said very confidently.

"Wow." McKenzie started in, "I thought you would never go back there."

"Yeah, well I thought I never would either, but the truth is I love that place and I love the memories that are there for me."

"You can stay here if you would like to, it would be fun for me to have the three of us together." Presscott suggested and McKenzie agreed.

"How about I stay here with you two and Jonathan on the weekends and I stay at the hotel during the week?"

Hannah asked.

"Well it seems like the heffa done thought this through." McKenzie said through a nervous laugh.

Presscott was hearing what her sister was not saying, so she asked her, "Are you going back to work Han?"

"Yes." Hannah responded.

All three of them were quiet and all eyes were on Hannah.

"I think that is great Hannah, but when did you decide all of this? You know we don't make these kinds of decisions without talking to one another." McKenzie said very attentively.

"I know. Presscott did not tell you this, but two nights before the brunch after everyone was asleep, I came over here and crawled into bed with her crying."

"Let me guess," McKenzie said with a roll of her eyes, "It was something your mother did or said that had you messed up."

Hannah averted her eyes to the couch trying to avoid Presscott.

"It's okay Hannah, you don't have to protect me." Presscott said giving her a comforting smile.

"Mudear was being herself and I did not want to deal with her anymore. By the way Scottie, I really do not care what kind of game Mudear is trying play with us concerning your paternity, you are the oldest Ellington child."

With that being said McKenzie raised her wine glass to her sisters and they toasted the two wine glasses and the one bottled water together and took a drink.

Hannah continued, "So after everything went down at the brunch I decided that the grieving process was over for me and I needed to move on."

"Well I am proud of you and if you need anything call me." McKenzie said with an approving smile.

"Thank you Kennie." Hannah responded and then all eyes were on Presscott.

"I am proud of you too, and if this is what you really want then I am behind you. I am so glad that you came to these conclusions on your own. Are you going to change the mansion any?" Presscott asked.

"What does that have to do with anything Scottie? Our sister has decided to move on with her life, don't psycho analyze this too." McKenzie said as a matter of fact.

"Kennie it is my job to analyze, besides and I quote 'heffa done made up her mind.'" Presscott looked at McKenzie like she dared her to say something.

A beat or two passed and Presscott continued in a loving voice, "Hannah my concern is everything on the property is programmed to respond with Anthony's voice being heard. Are you prepared for that?" Presscott said dismissing any attention that wanted to be given to McKenzie.

"Yes I did remember that and that is why I am staying at the Ritz Carlton until my house is completed." Hannah explained.

They then discussed all of the details of the Johnson Estate and Hannah going back to work.

"Hannah this is exciting with Ellington-Spencer working on your house, Halcyon and Sean will be thrilled." McKenzie started and then she continued with, "But Scottie I have some concerns about you."

Presscott was attentive because she wanted to be able to process her sister's concerns appropriately. "How are you doing? In spite of everything, have you been able to process any of this mess?"

Presscott began with her usual breath and then she said, "No, not really. I have not given too much mental energy to all of this. Once I got to Jonathan and told him what was disclosed that day, he reassured me that he loved me for me, and not my status in society. We also had some immediate solutions for me."

Both of the sisters looked concerned and they wanted to know what the immediate solutions were.

"Are you going to leave us?" Hannah asked with all sincerity.

"I would never leave my sisters." Presscott reassured them both and then continued, "After Halcyon and Sean return to Atlanta and get settled into Spencer Manor, I will start spending a lot of time in Virginia with Jonathan's family."

Hannah let out a sigh then sat in between her two sisters on the couch.

"I knew this was going to happen." McKenzie said with no emotion.

Hannah laid across her sisters' legs with her head in Presscott's lap.

"What's happening Kennie?" Presscott inquired.

"What has 'happened' is yo mamma has beaten you down so much that are going to gradually disappear from this family completely." McKenzie started to grow very sad in her voice.

"Kennie I will admit that I don't want anything else to do with Mudear, but the fact remains that she is my mother. I will always love and respect her as such. I am 32 years old and I have never had my mother love me the way a mother should love her child. Every time I see Jonathan's mother she always just loves on me and I need that."

With that expressed McKenzie said, "And there you have it folks, the great Elizabeth Ellington has found a way to make the oldest Ellington child excommunicate herself from the family." Then McKenzie twirled her index finger in the air with a mock celebration.

"No, no, no Kennie, you are missing the point. I have someone that wants to love me, like a mother and I am now taking her up on the offer." Presscott tried to explain.

"Where does that leave the remaining three sisters with you gone? Don't you get it? We are nothing without you." McKenzie tried to play the guilt card to no avail.

Presscott did not like having conversations like this even though she knew there was no way around it.

"No selfish Kennie," Hannah began to lend her thoughts to the conversation, "The one thing Mudear did do was show three of her children love. Scottie was depraved of that. There is nothing we can do to fix that, not even the love Scottie feels from Jonathan's mother can fix that. I think this is God's way of mending the hole in Scottie's heart. I commend her for taking you on Mrs. Chandler, I just request that I have access to you whenever I want."

Presscott brushed Hannah's hair away from her eyes and said, "I hope you all know that Jonathan and I would have it no other way. He has loved you guys from day one."

"Well..." McKenzie began.

Hannah cut off McKenzie with, "Well nothing Kennie. You are just selfish and the fact that someone else will be getting quality time from Scottie is wearing you out." Hannah was in a mood that the sisters had not seen since Anthony died.

Presscott loved this banter between the sisters, even though it was at McKenzie expense.

McKenzie pinched Hannah's calf playfully to get her to stop talking.

Hannah gave Presscott three examples of how McKenzie was extremely selfish when it came to Presscott.

All three of them laughed a little and Presscott even got a little teary eyed as she realized how much she loved her sisters. With everything being said they all agreed that maybe it was time for an outside source to intervene.

"Oh Scottie, I forgot to tell you something." McKenzie blurted out.

"What is it love?"

"You're getting a house guess tomorrow."

"Who?"

"Lance."

"Lance?"

"Yes."

"The New York realtor?"

"Yes."

"Huh…"

"Are we okay?"

"We shouldn't be…no proposals."

"Okay."

"Please understand what I am saying, if I get one proposal that it is the day that you get a condo in Buckhead."

"Okay."

"McKenzie Nicole Ellington I am not playing with you."

"Okay."

"Then we're okay."

"Oh Kennie you are so moving." Hannah was just saying.

nine:

It was the third day of Sean and Halcyon's honeymoon and they finally consummated their union. It was not a great experience for Halcyon and she wanted to analyze what had just taken place with Sean but he was fast asleep.

So she ran a bubble bath and analyzed it herself. Her thoughts immediately went to Presscott's advice, "Don't expect what you have seen in the movies, on television, or even what you may have heard in conversation. Don't expect anything, just be mentally present. Allow the love that you have for Sean to be the only thing present."

Then she heard McKenzie in her head, "It is going to hurt like hell baby girl!" Halcyon laughed and said out loud to herself, "Kennie you were so right."

Halcyon then became very quiet within herself as she remembered what Hannah said, "It probably will hurt like hell the first time, the second time, the third time and every time until your body gets used to it. The only thing I can guarantee you is that your love will grow for him. You guys are going about this according to the Bible and, therefore, only blessings can come out of this."

Halcyon's mind was not present, she is such a private and analytical person that she didn't know where her thoughts should be. Sean would never hurt her but this day he broke her body down. He was extremely gentle because he was very aware that her body was trembling. The initial penetration caused tears to escape from her eyes. Eventually Sean just stopped moving and once Halcyon caught her breath she began to move. She wanted to say something to him but she did not know what to say, so she said nothing. Sean climaxed and that was it, just like that it was over. Halcyon looked at the clock and thought, "That was the absolute longest ten minutes of my life."

Then she focused on what was good. She loved the way his skin felt against hers and even as she thought about it she blushed. She thought of the foreplay that was incredible, even as she thought about it a verbal, "Wow," escaped from her lips.

Hannah was right, Halcyon's love for her husband did grow.

Halcyon woke Sean by rubbing her bare leg against his calf gently. He tried to stop her by grabbing her foot but that only encouraged her to continue with a smile.

"Baby no, that's annoying." Sean said with his eyes still closed.

She stopped and he responded with a slightly irritable, "Thank you."

She then took her big toe and rubbed it up the back of his thigh. He was definitely awake and ready to play.

He grabbed her foot and pulled her body towards his and acted like he was going to bite her big toe. Halcyon stretched out her arms in an attempt to stop him and whispered, "Ow, ow, ow ..." She did not realize how sore her body was, but Sean was ready to play.

Halcyon cleared her throat and said very audibly, "No Sean that really hurts."

Sean turned the playfulness off and looked Halcyon in her face. He saw that she was serious and then he asked, "Is this from what we did?"

Halcyon did not want to say yes, but the truth was her pain was from what they did.

Then he asked her, "Where does it hurt?"

She swallowed hard and said, "Everywhere."

He put a smirk on his face and said, "Everywhere? That's impossible Mrs. Spencer."

She laughed and then said, "Ow, it even hurts to laugh."

"Well if I kiss it, will that make it better?" Sean asked with a hidden agenda.

"Maybe it will, maybe it won't, try it and see Mr. Spencer."

Halcyon was feeling pretty confident.

Sean balanced himself on his knees and opened Halcyon's robe to look at her body. His urge to touch her went away because he wanted to burn the vision of her perfect body in his mind's eye.

This session of foreplay was on another level, they didn't speak; they were very aware of one another. Halcyon often grimaced and moaned in pain, but this was something different. She wanted to experience whatever she needed to experience right there in that particular moment in time.

Sean was a gentleman and allowed her to express what she wanted to do and feel.

Everything seemed to be moving in slow motion.

The penetration was smoother. The body rhythm was synchronized. The kisses were sweeter. Nothing was awkward. Their backs arched away from one another but they were connected. Halcyon noticed that when she closed her eyes the sensual sensations were intensified.

Sean licked, kissed, sucked and nibbled everything possible. Nothing was rushed in the great exploration of their bodies. She discovered extremely sensitive areas on Sean. They were both attentive to one another.

Then they both climaxed together.

She collapsed into his chest. They lay there in the tightest embrace possible and nothing else existed.

Halcyon wanted this to become the usual for her, she wanted to always be excited; and Sean always wanted to feel this close and in love with her.

ten:

Jonathan returned home two days after Presscott. Then Nonny, Jonathan's mother arrived two days after Jonathan. She was a lady of class, she held her head up high and she never made anyone feel like they were beneath her.

Nonny showed up unannounced because she was on a mission. Her son, Jonathan, had always talked to her about Presscott's issues with Mudear. With this last incident she felt the need to check in on her lovely "Butterfly," Presscott herself. Nonny was always appalled at the way Mudear treated Presscott but now that she knew why, she needed to look in Mudear's face herself.

Nonny remembered how cold Mudear was to her at all of the Ellington girls' weddings.

Mudear once pulled Nonny to the side and asked her, "Why do you attempt to be a part of my family?"

Nonny answered her with a smile, "I have to by default; as a parent, sometimes you have to put up with shit you don't care to see or smell. This is done for the great love that I have for my Butterfly and my son. This is important to them and as a mother I suffer through it with a smile. Of course you would not know anything about motherly love now would you?"

Nonny never bit her tongue about anything and she never apologized for the words that she spoke. She was just Naomi Chandler and she just so happened to adore Presscott as her own.

When Nonny got to the Chandler Mansion, she stopped in the foyer to admire the new art work that was recently installed. As she was admiring one painting in particular, she was distracted in the entrance by McKenzie and some fella.

When McKenzie realized that Nonny was standing in the foyer she became elated. McKenzie hugged Nonny tightly and then she said, "You are a sight for sore eyes. I love you."

"I love you too baby, you are so precious to me and who is this fella?" Nonny asked without skipping a beat.

"Oh I apologize," McKenzie began and then said, "This is Lance."

"The New York realtor?" Nonny asked.

Lance immediately stepped up and declared, "That would be me in the flesh honey."

"Huh." Was Nonny's only response.

Everyone had their own way of trying to fix the situation between Mudear and Presscott. Hannah would busy herself at her law firm trying to find out all of the details about the rape.

Jonathan and Presscott decided to do nothing and allow Nonny to do what she was going to do.

Halcyon did not know yet, and the Ellington girls did not want to tell her without a resolution in place.

Without knowing it, McKenzie came up with the most dangerous way of dealing with Mudear.

"Hey daddy, are you busy?" McKenzie called Mr. Ellington on his cell phone.

"I'm never so busy that I can't talk to you. What's the topic for the day?" Mr. Ellington was so thrilled to be talking to his daughter because she seemed unusually distant since she had been in town for the wedding.

"Well the topic of the day is we need to have lunch at Einstein's." McKenzie had more than lunch on her mind.

"Absolutely, should I come and get you or do you want to meet me there?" Mr. Ellington said as he wrote a note to his secretary to clear his schedule for the remainder of the day.

"I will meet you there. Right now I'm out with Han, Scottie, Lance and Nonny and I don't know where I will be." McKenzie mentioned Nonny's name on purpose to peak her father's interest and it did.

"Nonny? What is she doing here?" Mr. Ellington became very attentive to the conversation that he was having with his daughter.

"I will tell you all about it when I see you." McKenzie felt like she dropped enough morsels for her father to nibble on.

"Okay McKenzie, then I will see you at 2:30," with that Mr. Ellington pushed the end button on his cell phone.

Mudear was busy about the estate making plans for a Multiple Sclerosis charity event when the butler announced that Mrs. Nonny Chandler was there to see her.

Mudear was shocked and disturbed by this announcement. She asked the butler to seat Nonny in the informal conference room but Nonny entered into Mudear's office uninvited,

"That's unnecessary, I'm right here." Nonny said pissed off.

Mudear and Nonny's eyes locked and Mudear began to give instructions to everyone that was in her office. Once the office was cleared Mudear began the conversation with a question, "Why on earth are you here?"

Nonny did not answer her immediately, she just looked at her intently trying to make since of what made her tick. Nonny finally said, "I came to town because my son told me what you did to my Butterfly. Personally I did not believe that not even you could be that evil so I just needed to come and look at you for myself.

Mudear's heart began to melt just a little but not enough to be vulnerable to Nonny Chandler.

"Is all of that true Elizabeth?" Nonny said staring right into Mudear's eyes. "Is it true that you don't know who your oldest child's father is?" Nonny was very straight forward with Mudear.

"Yes." Mudear said with no emotion.

"Is it true that you were brutally raped and that's why the paternity of your child is questionable?" Nonny just wanted to get to the bottom of this.

"Yes." Mudear answered again, still no emotion. Mudear was tired of running from how she treated Presscott; she did not know how to sort through the years of pain.

Then Nonny asked Mudear as she stepped around her desk and got face to face with her, "Why is Butterfly paying for this shit?"

Mudear straightened her back and prepared for battle, "Because she might be the result of something that broke me."

Those words cut Nonny's heart into a million pieces.

Nonny stepped away from Mudear just watching her and then she sat at a table that was across the room.

"Do you have any more questions for me Mrs. Chandler?" Mudear asked feeling like she just won her first battle against Nonny.

"Elizabeth, come have a seat with me over here because this is far from being over today. I am not leaving until my heart tells me that it's time to go. You cannot easily get over on me like you do with my Butterfly. Around you her wings are clipped. How is it that your grown ass don't know who your daughter's daddy is?" Nonny was trying to control her anger.

Mudear walked to the front of her desk and leaned on it for support then said, "Understand, what happened to me was vicious and evil and Presscott has always taken me back to that week."

"What happened to you was vicious and evil." Nonny repeated in efforts to make a point. "And because of that you treat an innocent child who might be the result of this vicious and evil act, viciously and evil? What the hell is your problem? Did you enjoy being treated that way?"

Mudear was appalled by the insinuation and she answered as such, "No, I did not enjoy being treated that way and how dare you presume that I did."

"It's not a presumption Elizabeth, I am merely acting

on the facts that I know and drawing a conclusion. I was raped as well and I did not rest until justice was served on the individual that committed such a vicious and evil act against me." Nonny explained.

"Well." Mudear began, "I was very much in love with my perpetrator at one point in time in my life. We had plans of marriage and children and undeniable happiness."

Nonny let out a sigh and said, "That still does not explain to me why you treat your baby the way you do. I am not here to pass judgment, I am just trying to understand your chain of thinking. You see, when you are in a mode of 'let me crush Presscott' I'm the one who gets the calls with no words just sobs. If you really loved that baby you would stop all of this nonsense."

Mudear took a deep breath and said very sternly, "I never said that I loved Presscott."

"Okay, okay, okay..." Nonny said as she stood up, "My heart just told me that it is time to leave, so that's what I will do. But before I go I need to tell you something from Naomi to Elizabeth." Nonny walked over to Mudear and hugged her and said, "This is not your fault. I understand what's going on inside of you. This is not your fault. Call me whenever you need to."

Mudear wanted to hug Nonny back with a sigh of

relief. Instead she adorned her victorious smirk at the corner of her mouth and then summoned for all of her workers to return back to her office.

Nonny put on her shades and left saying out loud to herself through anger, "Oh yours is coming special bitch and I pray it's through me."

eleven:

"So, dear McKenzie, do you know how much Daddy loves you?" Mr. Ellington asked as McKenzie walked into the private dining area for two.

McKenzie walked over to her father and gave him a big hug and a kiss. She loved her father so much and often wondered what he saw in Mudear.

The waiter came in the dining room and took their drink orders. When the waiter left the dining room McKenzie jumped into the reason why she wanted to meet with her father. "Dad," McKenzie began, "Your wife has really done it this time."

"Before you start in on Mudear, you mentioned someone named Lance. Who is Lance?" Mr. Ellington asked.

"He is a friend of mine who is going to help with Spencer Manor." That was a lie and she didn't know why she lied to her father.

"The New York realtor?" He asked

"Yes." She responded truthfully.

"Huh," was Mr. Ellington's only response and then he beckoned McKenzie to carry on with her story.

"She told all of us at brunch that she didn't know who Scottie's daddy was. Nonny came to town to talk to your wife but I don't think that will change anything. Now Jonathan is going to move Scottie to Virginia so Nonny can be the mother that Scottie never had. I bet your wife didn't tell you that!" McKenzie said all of that in one breath.

Mr. Ellington started to get a headache because he felt his passive state of dealing with his family ending but he needed to know some things before he began to move into action. "How is Presscott doing?" was Mr. Ellington's first question.

"She's coping. She is always strong in front of us but I can only imagine the breakdown that Jonathan is going to have to endure." McKenzie was ready to answer anything that her father wanted to know.

"How are you and Hannah holding up?" He asked with great concern.

"I am going to be honest I am trying to stay as far away from your wife as possible because I really want to hurt her really bad. Hannah is back to work because she taped the conversation, and she wants to investigate everything your wife said. I can tell you that we all have been extremely hurt by this and I just keep thinking that this seems out of your wife's evil league. Something is definitely up."

The waiter re-entered the dining room and took the

food orders. When the waiter left, Mr. Ellington looked into McKenzie's eyes and said, "There is an appropriate place of anger towards Mudear but I truly believe this is my fault."

McKenzie brushed off her father's statement because there was no way that he had anything to do with this, but she entertained his words anyway, "What do you mean?" she asked with mock perplexity.

"What I mean is that maybe I should talk to my four girls together because there is so much to tell." Mr. Ellington was trying to figure out how to buy some time.

McKenzie did not like the weight of these words that her father was saying, so she asked him, "Can you tell me if the rape is true and could Presscott have another father?"

Mr. Ellington took a drink of his lemonade and said, "McKenzie, Mudear was brutally raped for seven days by a man that we both knew from high school and yes there was a strong possibility that Presscott may not be my biological child."

McKenzie was becoming heart broken and angry all at the same time. She stared at her reflection in the plate on the table and asked, "Do you know who Presscott's father is?"

Mr. Ellington leaned back in his chair and answered,

"Maybe I do."

McKenzie stood up, picked up her purse and said, "Wow, Stanley, the better answer would have been no. It's not fair for her to have turned out to be such a great person, and have the most f'd up parents to show for it. Here's a news flash for you, Presscott is a real breathing person with a golden heart made of flesh. I don't understand why the two most messed up people on earth were chosen to be her parents." McKenzie knew she had only scratched the surface of something much deeper but she walked out of the restaurant and to her car. Her thoughts were all over the place and she could not fathom how the outcome was going to be.

twelve:

Stanley and Elizabeth sat at their dining room table at the main estate. Stanley looked worn out from going to meeting after meeting and Elizabeth just looked gorgeous. As they ate dinner the conversation was typical until Stanley asked, "Guess who I had lunch with yesterday?"

Mudear felt no caution when he told her McKenzie. Stanley questioned Mudear about the conversation during the brunch. When Mudear admitted that she told her daughters about the rape, Stanley instantly dropped his fork and slapped Mudear with the back of his hand across her jaw.

She had just taken a bite of her food, so the food flew out of her mouth. She remained sitting in her chair and she guided her look slowly back to his face. "I guess this redeems your manhood." Mudear said with no emotions.

Stanley raised his hand again and slapped her again in the same spot. This time the pain registered and blood trickled out of her mouth. They spoke to each other calmly as Mudear wiped her mouth.

"Why do you insist on breaking down my child every chance you get?"

"She represents the woman I want to be."

"It's not her fault that you are not who you want to be."

"No. It's her father's fault."

"What?"

"I have allowed you to cause all of my children to hate me."

Stanley raised his hand to slap Mudear again. This time she stopped the motion of his hand with her own. She grabbed his throat with both of her hands and began choking him. He tried to pry her hands off his throat.

Mudear said to him very quietly, "This is the last time you try to break me." She released her grip and began walking out of the dining room.

Stanley got up and followed Elizabeth down the hall. When he reached her he grabbed her arm and spun her around to face him. She was terrified but she couldn't show it. Mudear would not allow her eyes to stop staring into his.

"I wonder what Kennie would do if she saw her daddy roughing up Mudear?" Elizabeth was trying to find any rabbit in the hat that would stop Stanley from violently proceeding.

Stanley in one move slung Mudear against the wall and held her there with his forearm, "Keep Kennie out of this." He demanded through clenched teeth.

"Stanley one day the truth will come out, and I think it's in the very near future." Mudear's words were greeted with another hit across her face which was followed by a barrage of hits across her beautiful face.

With the last hit Mudear tried to stay conscious as she slid down the wall. She kept thinking to herself, *if he kills me this time, my face has to be presentable because he will beat my corpse for not being properly suitable for viewing while I'm dead.*

Elizabeth parked her car about a block away from Presscott's house. She looked through the numbers in her cell phone. She found the number she was looking for and hesitated to make the call. Elizabeth activated the number and cleared her throat. The voice answered with hello, Elizabeth began to quietly sob.

Naomi repeatedly said hello and then she heard, "I apologize for calling you like this."

"Elizabeth where are you." Naomi asked with great concern.

"I'm just outside the Chandler Mansion." She said between breaths.

"I will be right there. Don't hang up okay?" she asked.

Elizabeth agreed.

Naomi left the house unannounced. She immediately found the car. Naomi walked up to the driver side of the car and when she saw Mudear's face she covered her mouth in shock by what she saw. "Open this door right now," Naomi demanded.

Elizabeth opened the door and allowed her head to bow in shame.

Naomi sat in the frame of the door and closely inspected Elizabeth's face then she asked, "Honey who happened to your face?"

"Stanley," she whispered.

Naomi repeated Stanley's name just to be sure she heard her correctly. "Move over. I'm driving." Naomi insisted.

Elizabeth didn't pay attention to where they were going.

The Chandlers had relatives that lived in Atlanta that were doctors and Naomi knew she could trust them with secrecy on this matter. She drove to the Kaniawa sub division in Stone Mountain and she started out just listening to Elizabeth randomly talk.

Elizabeth "Mudear" Ellington never wanted to admit to anyone that Stanley was physically abusive to her. After she spoke to Naomi "Nonny" Chandler in her office about Presscott, a kindred spirit was woven between the two.

Elizabeth never dreamed that Nonny would be the one that she would run to when another episode of the abuse occurred. This time though, Elizabeth had to admit that the hits seemed worse than before. The hits were few but bone altering. In her mind her face wasn't that bad but even Nonny immediately knew that she had multiple broken bones in her face.

Nonny made sure Elizabeth was conscious even while Nonny drove her around. Mentally, Elizabeth came to grips with the fact that she was going to have to have a portion of her face reconstructed and she nursed the urge to apologize for making Stanley so angry. McKenzie was the only child that would *tell* on Mudear. Whatever McKenzie had to tell, Mudear was beaten by her husband as a result. The two of them butted heads the first time she held her in her arms. The first day McKenzie was at the Estate and Mudear laid her down for a nap, Stanley threatened her with the notion that if McKenzie didn't get the best of her love, he would kill her.

"Well it's been thirty years now," Mudear contemplated in a whisper, "maybe it's time to die." Mudear didn't want to be beat to death; she wanted all of her daughters to know that she really did love them and wanted them to know the truth about everything, except the abuse. She never wanted them to have ill thoughts towards their father that's why she always allowed her children to think the worst of her. Stanley loved his daughters and Mudear didn't want anything to come between them.

"I don't understand." Nonny said as she drove.

"What?" Mudear asked.

"You put up this façade like you are untouchable but you let Stanley wup yo ass like this. I don't understand." Nonny was baffled.

Mudear chuckled. "Yeah well," she began, "the first time he did this I fought back and that's when he taught me to do what he says. I didn't forget the lesson. I never fought back again before tonight. Ironically enough, I love him something deep so I would never report him. I would lie on the witness stand under oath to protect him."

"Chile then I say your intelligence is skin deep and your smarts don't even come close to that."

They both laughed.

Mudear let out a painful groan as she tried not to smile when she laughed. She understood that her new friend just called her dumb in a nice way, she agreed.

Nonny reached over and touched Mudear's shoulder and reassured her that everything was going to be okay.

Mudear then said, "Thank you for always being there

for Butterfly, she truly loves you. I apologize for causing her all the pain that you dealt with."

Nonny truly did not know how to respond to that because of all of the years of frustration and hate she had built up towards Mudear was deflated, wow.

They finally reached a gate to a beautiful property. She put in a code and the gate parted in the middle. By the time Naomi reached the side door, her cousin Kevin was there to greet her with a hug.

While in their embrace, Nonny said to him, "I need your help with something in the car."

By that time his wife walked to the door and greeted Naomi with a welcoming hug as well.

Kevin looked in the car and realized what the help was in the car, he began to give his wife instructions, "I'm going to need my medical bag and a pair of lady's pajamas in the downstairs guest room. Please notify my staff that we have an emergency here at the house."

Kevin opened the passenger door and said, "Hello, I'm Dr. Kevin Chandler. You are at my home. I need to get you out of the car. Are you okay with me carrying you or do you want to walk?"

Elizabeth grimaced as she spoke through clenched teeth, "I can walk." Elizabeth stepped out of the car and collapsed into Kevin's arms.

He carried her into the house and straight to the guest bedroom. When Kevin walked passed his wife, she gasped and prayed out loud for nothing to be broken.

Kevin stepped out of the guest room and got Nonny's attention and asked, "Who is this woman?"

"Elizabeth Ellington."

"No seriously, who is this woman?"

"Seriously, Elizabeth Ellington."

"So this is Stanley's handy work."

Now why did Kevin know that?

thirteen:

Hannah busied herself at her office trying to find every bit of information on the supposed rape that took place within the year Presscott was born. To her surprise there was nothing in the local papers, and nothing on archived news reports. Was this all a lie? Hannah showed up at the Ellington Estate unannounced and went straight to the family archives. She looked through everything that she thought might give her answers and there was nothing. She had spent two hours looking through file after file to no avail. She took her Chanel pumps off, unbuttoned her Chanel suit jacket and laid down on the floor staring at the ceiling. This would not give her any answers but it would help her clear her mind.

She looked across the floor to the right and saw something that did not register in her mind. Then she looked across the floor to her left and saw nothing out of place. She turned back to the right and squinted her eyes as she tried to make out the foreign object on the floor. Was it red or black and what was it?

Hannah got off of the floor and put her pumps back on and then made her way to the right side of the room. Everything in this room was either a manila color or a rust color so it should have been easy to find something either black or red, so she thought. She got on the floor again and looked for the object again and discovered that it was right in her face. It was a cabinet that had been painted to match everything in its area, the original color of the cabinet was red and the very bottom was left untouched for identification. The label on the front of the cabinet was blank but there was a label behind it with neat hand writing on it. Hannah pulled the label out and it read, "Elizabeth 1968." Hannah's heart dropped into her stomach because she found what she was looking for and was not sure if she really wanted to read the contents. She opened the cabinet and began to read the labels and one heading in particular caught her attention and it read, "Anthony Johnson." She opened that file and it had three dividers inside that read "Introduction," "Wedding," and "Death?" Hannah took that file and put it in her brief case. She walked back the cabinet and took the file that read, "Rape." She could not believe what her mother went through and maybe she was starting to understand her mother's actions. Hannah stared at the wall and tried to process the information that she was reading, she looked back down into the file cabinet and a yellow folder caught her attention. The label on it read, "Paternity Test," and the moisture in Hannah's mouth evaporated immediately.

She put all of the files back and paced the length of the archive room trying to decide if she should find out the paternity of her sister. Hannah took a deep breath and massaged her temples and then went back to the cabinet and picked up the yellow folder. She read the results and refused to have any emotion and she knew that she would not be staying at the hotel this night; she was going straight to the Chandler Mansion. Hannah took all of the files that pertained to her sisters and put them in her briefcase. Hannah got in her car and called Presscott. They had a brief conversation and then Presscott agreed to meet her sister at the railroad tracks. When Hannah hung up from Presscott she called McKenzie and the three of them were in route to Flowers Road.

fourteen:

Remington Williams was a senior partner at the prestigious Ellington-Johnson law firm. The dreadlocked Adonis was Corbin Wolfe. He was a junior partner at the firm. He caught her off guard as she walked down the hall at work one afternoon. He decided to try and sneak a kiss while she really wasn't paying attention, but she was always paying attention. She was digging him in a major way but she wasn't going to act on it because then she would be breaking her own rule, don't date where you work. So now she stood in the hallway with him faced with a challenge that she wanted to desperately answer.

"Hey lady." He leaned in real close for a kiss.

She moved her head slightly out of the way and whispered in his ear, "This is not the time, nor the place." She stepped away from him and continued walking down the hall severely fighting the urge of looking back.

What did that mean? He really wanted to know.

When she reached her desk, her computer indicated that she had a new inner office email. She looked at the sender's name, took a deep breath and decided to remain professional. The email simply read, "Your place or mine and what time?"

She quickly responded, "Please DO NOT email me

again unless it is pertaining to work. If you do email me again and it does not pertain to work I will contact H.R. immediately. Thank you for your cooperation."

When she activated the send toggle on her computer the intercom sounded with a soft tone and her secretary announced her best friend, Hannah, was on the line. She picked up the receiver and explained that she would not be in attendance at ladies night because something came up at the last minute concerning work and she had to take care of it.

During her conversation with her best friend she was composing a note to HIM pertaining to time and place.

At 7:30 pm she was sitting at Twist waiting for him to show for their meeting. At 7:32 pm he stood trying to figure out the purpose of their meeting. She stood and shared a brief professional greeting and indicated to the hostess that she was ready to be seated. They talked momentarily and then she asked, "What's your cell number?" Her gaze never left his eyes as she input his number without looking at her key pad on her cell phone. Then she said without hesitation or thought, "Place, yours...time, now." He paid for the drinks that were not touched at 7:52 pm. She followed him to his place while they engaged in an erotic conversation on their cell phones.

When they arrived at his condo in Cabbage Town, words were not spoken. She only noticed how the condo appeared to be tidy, how his lips pressed against her lips gently, and how his hands had a language of their own. The kiss was comforting and had the taste of sweet nectar. She liked how her body concaved to his embrace as his convexed over her's. He carried her to his bedroom and sat her on the edge of his bed.

"May I undress you?" It was his polite, gentle and sensual request of her.

She wanted to do this and get it over with, she didn't want any conversation. But to her surprise she answered with a welcoming and breathless yes.

The way he undressed her was climactic and she had never felt more desirable in her life.

Their eyes locked as he undressed her. He picked her up and placed her in the center of the bed on her back. She tried to reason herself out of pleasure but every one of her attempts was met with a counter attempt from him which was done in a non-aggressive way.

The original penetration was gentle and smooth which caused every wall that she had up to melt away. She fought hard to exist only in her head but by the time the second thrust was introduced she was all his. Whatever he wanted and needed she was willing to give without question. She allowed him to do things to her that she never thought of, things that she only dreamed about and was afraid to inquire about. She did them to him as well. They had never been on a date, there had only been innocent flirting at work. Where did this come from?

Afterwards in a deep sleep in the unfamiliar place and resting easy, her eyes opened wide then rested at a squint. She grabbed at the bed because she needed to hold on to something. She was going on an unexpected ride really fast and she just needed to hold on. She tried to get in her head for a moment so she could figure out what was happening. Her back arched away from the bed and then she realized what he was doing to her. She had never felt it quite like this before. Her entire body shivered involuntarily. His tongue was warm between her thighs and she did not have time to fight it.

There it was, the best orgasm she had ever had. She wanted to do something for him but all she could do was breathe.

Slowly.

Inhale.

Hold.

Exhale.

She laid there on her back and tears escaped from her eyes and hit the pillow in a constant flow.

This was the lady's first night with the dreadlocked Adonis that caused her to break all of her personal rules of engagement. Also on this night she broke the unthinkable rule with her best friend. She lied to her.

When she drove home she thought of how to confess. She wondered if she needed to say anything at all but lying was not her forte. She knew that this would not be her last encounter with him. Her thoughts went to the events that had occurred that evening; a mischievous grin rested on her face. As she pulled into her driveway the grin was traded for a look of perplexity. She kept hearing in her head, "Her no meant yes."

Her thoughts were interrupted by her cell phone ringing, she answered gently, "Hello."

"Hey girl."

"Hey, good morning."

"Good morning to you too. I'm on my way over with breakfast, is that okay?"

"Yep, use your key. I'm headed to the shower."

"Okay, see you shortly."

Hannah noted to herself that Remington was in the car. Was she just leaving work? Huh.

Presscott heard McKenzie call to her from her bedroom doorway, "Scottie, are you up here?"

"In my closet," Presscott yelled towards the door.

McKenzie walked into the closet and marveled at its enormity and then said, "This is not a closet Scottie, this is a luxury apartment."

"Huh, said the woman who has an entire floor in an apartment building dedicated to be her personal coffre." Presscott smiled at her sister and then said, "Come have a seat on the chase and let's talk."

McKenzie crossed over to the chase in the closet. She sat down and leaned back on her arms and asked Presscott, "What do you do in her?"

"Well right now I'm picking out five suits for the week because I decided to see patients."

"Oh really," McKenzie responded.

"Yeah girl, Mudear doesn't bother me when I'm at work."

They both found amusement in that statement because they knew it to be very true.

It was quiet for a brief moment and then McKenzie said, "Scottie I'm working on a theory."

Presscott turned to look at her sister and said, "Let me interrupt first."

"Okay. What's up?"

"I don't know how to say this to you Kennie."

"What? Just say the shit."

"Well, you have to buy a condo in Buckhead by the end of the week."

"Shut up, no I don't"

"The first proposal, I kinda let go. The second proposal was in front of Jonathan, down on one knee."

They couldn't help it, they both laughed.

"Speaking of which, where is Lance?"

"He's getting the grand tour of the Ellington grounds, compound and estate. What did JC do when Lance proposed?"

Presscott cleared her throat, bowed her head and tried to imitate Jonathan's voice, "Man get up and go somewhere out of my house wit dis shit."

"Oooo Scottie you lying cuz JC don't cuss."

"Them lies you tell, he doesn't cuss in the presence of women unless he is truly pissed off. He refuses to cuss in front of his mother or an Ellington, except me. His mother was there, that's all I'm saying."

"Damn. Scottie I am so sorry. Now what am I supposed to do with him?"

"Here's a thought, you do have a mansion on the estate."

McKenzie looked at Presscott pleading for another solution.

Presscott then said, "This one is on you babe. Now

I interrupted a theory you were about to share with me, what's up?"

McKenzie was upset. She brought Lance to Atlanta because of an impulse she had due to a conversation she had with him, now this.

Presscott sat next her sister seated on the chase, hugged her and then said, "This should not upset you like this, what's going on?"

"Well I have two things." McKenzie took a deep breath as she considered what she was about to say. "First, I don't think Mudear caused all of problems in our family by herself."

Presscott wanted to hear this theory so she asked, "What makes you say that Younger?"

"Remember when all of us were out shopping with Lance in tow and I had to go to a meeting?"

"I remember." Presscott answered.

"That meeting was with Stanley, your alleged father."

Presscott understood that McKenzie was really pissed off right now and her anger landed on dear ole dad because she referred to him by his first name. So Presscott didn't agitate McKenzie with questions, she just listened.

"I went to him to tell on your mother because I wanted her to be reprimanded. He showed no emotions or feelings when I talked about the brunch. He asked how all the girls were doing and then he said he should sit down with all of his girls and explain some things. When I asked him if he knew who your father was, he said, 'maybe'. What kind of hell response is that?"

Presscott still didn't say anything, she just raised an eyebrow.

"You know the more I think about this whole mess, I'm starting to believe that Mudear is the innocent. Stanley always comes out smelling like a bed of roses. Have you noticed that we haven't seen or heard from Mudear in a couple of days? Something ain't right Scottie and I intend to figure this one out."

Presscott stood up and began playing with a button on one of her suits for a moment and then she finally spoke, "McKenzie our family is a very complexed one to say the least. Now if we're going to start rattling trees, especially old ones, you are going to have to be able to remove yourself from it. Family hurts are debilitating. Do you really think you can handle what you may or may not discover about daddy?"

McKenzie smiled and said, "Of course I can, you said we."

Presscott walked up to her sister without a smile on her face and said, "My help is coming with a condition this time."

McKenzie didn't like this side of Presscott. She took a step back and said, "Damn Scottie what's the condition?"

"When we finish with our family," she began, "then we go to New York and dig around in Michael's backyard."

"Well your line of thinking is my number two." McKenzie just stared at the floor because she knew whatever the truth was concerning Michael; it was going to crush her.

"I'm listening," Presscott said as she tried to interpret her sister's raw emotions, as of right now things were not adding up.

"Remember how I told you I saw Michael sexing one of my student/instructors?"

"Yes."

"Well apparently Sammy and Lance looked into it and it was two look a likes that got paid to do that."

"Why?"

"I don't know. I brought Lance here hoping he could meet with you and Hannah to try and get to the bottom of this."

"Okay." Presscott tapped her chin three times and then said, "Call Lance and have him to meet us at my office in Dunwoody. I want to talk to him before we bring

bring Hannah in on this."

McKenzie took out her cell phone and spoke the command into it to, *call Lance.*

"Hey." Presscott said in a whisper.

McKenzie turned to face her sister with a question on her face.

Presscott motioned for her sister to walk towards her and she opened her arms wide.

McKenzie spoke into her cell phone asking, "Can you hold for me?"

The two sisters embraced tenderly with Presscott saying in a whisper, "I love you."

McKenzie responded with, "Thank you. I love you too."

Presscott knew they were waging a war and the enemy may not be Mudear this time.

fifteen:

Hannah, being an attorney and having to deal with her mother on a regular basis, walked into Remington's house and felt a lie hanging in the air.

This was a typical morning between the two friends. They always caught up with one another's personal lives at one another's house for breakfast

Remington was worried about how this particular morning was going to go because she was not at work like she claimed. Did her best friend already know that?

Hannah walked into the kitchen wondering if she could handle Remington's lie. She needed her help in figuring out what to do about Mudear. She put on a pot of coffee, planted a "tell all brownie" and looked at her watch. She made a mental note of the time down to the second.

She went to the living room and turned the T.V. to Good Morning America and programmed the inner picture to CSNBC. Hannah knew she had to be creative, sensitive and right when she dealt with Mudear.

She stood in front of the T.V. screen not paying attention to any of the content. The smell of the coffee brought her back to being in Remington's house. She made herself a cup of coffee and then stood in front of the bay window that overlooked Buckhead. It was something beautiful to see.

Then Hannah heard, "Hey girl, how is everything this mo'nin?" Remmington asked her friend.

Hannah stole a glance at her watch. She quickly calculated the time in her head as she answered without skipping a beat, "It's been really crazy," Hannah smiled to herself as she thought *seventeen minutes and eight seconds. This lie is about sex with someone she doesn't want me to know about.*

Remington poured herself a cup of coffee and yelled to Hannah from the kitchen, "Come in here Joe."

Hannah walked into the kitchen, they switched coffee mugs and the conversation began about what Hannah had been discovering about Mudear.

Remmington devoured the "tell all brownie," *this sex was exceptionally good sex.*

THE NEXT DAY

Hannah awoke in the hotel suite with an uneasy feeling. She lay in bed haphazardly tossing and turning trying to shake the turmoil she felt for about an hour. Finally getting out of bed Hannah took a nice long hot shower, that didn't help the uneasiness. She looked at the clock; it read 10:47 am. Hannah called the firm to let them know that she would be working out of the office and she would be on mobile access all day. She put on her most comfortable jogging suite and packed up her laptop, phone and all of the accessories. She went to the lobby and requested the use of a private dining room all day. An attendee led her along with her bodyguard to a midsized dining room and on his departure she gave him a one hundred dollar bill for his pocket, ten dollars for a large Caramel Maquiota from Starbucks with soy milk, extra caramel and a menu from the hotel kitchen. The attendee left to assist with Hannah's request as she set up her work space. As she sat in front of her computer waiting to log onto the internet, her cell phone rang. She answered with the earpiece and without identifying the caller:

"Hello."

"Hi. I'm trying to reach Hannah Johnson."

"This is she."

"How are you doing today?"

"Well. I hope things are well with you. Who is this?"

"I have always loved how you get to the point."

"Detective David Brendel is that you?"

"It's me."

"How can I assist you detective?"

"Can't say over the phone; it's pretty sensitive. Can we meet somewhere today?"

"3434 Peachtree Rd. Ask for me at the front desk."

"I will be there in fifteen minutes."

"Okay."

Disconnect.

The turmoil inside Hannah intensified. A knock came at the door and the attendee entered with the Starbucks and the menu. She then informed him that a Mr. David Brendel was coming to meet with her. She asked that he be escorted to the conference room. She walked over to her computer and began to do a search on David's most recent cases. All but two cases were successfully closed, one was Anthony Johnson and the other was Kiki Combs.

As she skimmed through Kiki Combs' information, she called Remington on her cell phone:

"Hey boss, what's up?"

"Hey Remmy, are you in the office?"

"Yea what's wrong?"

"I don't know yet. Can you look up everything on Kiki Combs?"

"Kiki Combs? Wasn't she killed the same day Ant..." Remington's voice trailed off as she realized what she was about to ask Hannah. "Shit Joe that was insensitive of me. Hold on."

Then Hannah heard Remmington say, "Corbin I'm sorry I have to take this call, I will have my secretary send that information to you." Remmington sat down at her computer and asked, "What's going on Hannah?"

Hannah closed her eyes and started going over the day's events as she repeated them to Remington. Then Hannah said, "Detective David Brendel is coming to the hotel to talk to me about something sensitive. I pulled up all of his cases."

Remmington cut her off with, "I'm looking at it now, say no more. Just so you know the Combs family is on a pro bono retainer for anything as long as they want."

Hannah let out a sigh looking for relief but none was found, then she said, "Don't hang up the phone. I want you to hear the conversation and start working while we are talking."

Remmington simply said, "No worries, I'm muting my phone now."

Moments later a knock came at the door and the attendee announced Mr. David Brendel.

David entered the room offering Eddie Post, Hannah a swing of his fist in camaraderie. Eddie stepped to the side and disarmed the detective.

Eddie looked at the detective's weapon and asked, "Man when you gonna let me update this for you."

"When you quit and I get hired for your position." The detective responded quickly.

The banter between the friends could go on for hours so Hannah stepped in and said, "Okay you two. Detective you have a sensitive matter to discuss therefor Eddie we need some privacy."

Eddie gave a respectable nod of his head and left the room.

Hannah motioned for David to sit across from the computer and right in front of the hidden cell phone.

"So detective," Hannah began, "what's the sensitive matter that needs my attention?"

David studied Hannah for a moment and then he began to speak, "I have a case open for an eighteen year old girl named Kiki Combs. Your law firm holds the retainer for the family. They have instructed us to speak to you only."

Hannah just listened for now.

"We have reason to believe that she was killed by a serial killer and we have an idea of who it is thanks to the B.A.U. out of Quantico."

Hannah cleared her throat and asked, "How long have you had the idea of who this perpetrator is?"

The detective leaned back in his chair and folded his hands across his stomach. "Roughly about a year and a half, and you are just now hearing about this because you just now came back to work. I found that out two days ago, so now I'm here."

Hannah was satisfied with his answer so she raised her hands and shrugged her shoulders with acceptance. "Why was the Behavioral Analysis Unit brought in on this case?" She asked out of curiosity.

"Well," the detective reached into his inside jacket pocket and pulled out a number of photographs of teenaged girls and spread them out on the table. Then he began to explain: "The girls were killed on the fifteen of random months when they turned eighteen. They are all from wealthy families and you may notice that they all favor one another. Their families have all disappeared and the only thing in common is that they look like one another, even the style of hair and the birth day."

Hannah studied the pictures and the similarity of the looks began to bother her, they were too familiar. She continued to listen.

"The B.A.U. tracked a potential perpetrator but didn't have enough evidence to make an arrest. The person they were watching has taken himself through a complete metamorphosis. He now has locked hair. He went to law school and has the highest bar score in Atlanta."

Hannah interrupted him and said, "The gentleman with the highest bar score in Atlanta is employed at my firm. His name is..."

And all three of them said his name at the same time, "Corbin Wolfe."

"That's right." The detective said and continued with, "Corbin Wolfe and you, Mrs. Johnson know the young lady in this last picture. Who is this?"

Hannah looked at the picture and didn't want to identify the subject but indeed it was Halcyon on her eighteenth birthday, June 15th. Hannah stood up and began to pace as she answered, "That's my baby sister." Hannah stopped pacing and sat on the table and she lowered her face to the detective's and asked, "What is really going on?"

"Your sister and Mr. Wolfe went to Dunwoody Prep together. They were in the same senior class and they went to undergrad together; that seems to be the only connection that we found. Now Hannah listen to me, Mr. Wolfe has recently bedded someone that you are really close to. We think he is trying to get his prize, Halcyon, and maybe in the process sabotage your family any way that he can while he's in the process of doing so." He explained.

Hannah leaned back to let her feet dangle off of the table as she processed what he just said. She walked around the table and picked up her Starbucks and swallowed quickly, then she repeated, "He recently bedded someone that I'm really close to?" She considered all of the possibilities but could not come up with a definite so she asked, "Who did he sleep with that I'm really close to?"

The question wasn't completely out of her before he said the name Remmington Williams.

"Are you sure?" Hannah was baffled as she asked the question because he goes against the rule.

Hannah retrieved her cell phone.

"Yes," the detective answered and continued with, "I have their entire session in audio visional surround sound."

When Hannah looked back at the detective he was pulling out a disk from his inside jacket pocket.

Hannah got to her phone and began saying, "Remmy take your phone off mute."

Silence.

"Remmy I can see that we are still connected. Talk to me."

Silence.

Remington was crushed. She couldn't talk to Hannah, she didn't want to talk to Hannah. Remmington coupled her arms on top of her head in a feeble attempt to bury her head and then she heard Hannah say, "This is not the time to try and bury your head in the sand. Come on Rem I know you and I still love you. The brownie let the secret out at breakfast. Please take your phone off mute."

Hannah heard a sniffle and her heart eased just a little.

Remmington took a big breath and said, "Joe I'm sorry I should have told you."

Hannah's heart became heavy because she was not there to give her friend a hug.

"Remmy listen to me," Hannah began, "I promise everything is okay but I need you here with me. I'm sending the Post bird to pick you up at the nest okay?"

Hannah heard another deep breath but it was cut short. Then she heard a male voice talking to Remmington. "Miss Williams..."

With the sound of his voice Remmington turned to face Corbin and he noticed at once that she was upset. The gentleman side of him inquired, "Are you okay?"

"Hey Corbin," Remmington said.

Hannah immediately started feeding Remmington lines over the phone.

You're fine. Hannah then scribbled a note and walked it over to Eddie.

"I'm fine." Remmington stated.

"But you're crying." Corbin tried to gently nudge to get her to open up a little more.

Unexpected bad news, Hannah coached.

"I got some unexpected bad news and it threw me off my guard that's all," Remmington responded.

"Is there anything I can do to help?" Corbin asked sincerely.

You can die Hannah didn't realize that she said *that* thought out loud.

Remmington cleared her throat and the detective gave her a surprised look.

"Well Mr. Wolfe I have a situation unfolding right before my eyes and I don't know what to do about it." Remmington was angry with the whole situation and she didn't want her best friend figuring out this for her. "I don't know if you know this but Hannah Ellington Johnson and I have been the best of friends sense we were four years old. So literally there is no line of demarcation in our bloodlines."

Corbin had no idea of what she was talking about.

Hannah knew what Remmington was about to do so she tried to plead with her gently out of a confrontation.

"Are you aware of the one pro bono case that Mrs. Johnson is solo over?"

"Kiki Combs."

"You answered that too damned quick. Here's something you don't know." Remmington was pissed. "The B.A.U. has a copy of our sexual encounter because you are a suspect as a serial killer. Are you trying to kill the youngest Ellington?"

Corbin was trying to keep his cool as he simply answered, "No."

"If I find out you are lying to me so help me God, I will march you into Lenox Mall and execute you myself."

Corbin became amused with her threat and said, "You would never get away with that."

"I will always be considered an Ellington, I can get away with murdering you in public in Atlanta. No line of demarcation in the blood lines you idiot."

Right at that moment Remmington's office door was opened forcefully. She was extracted from her office. Corbin Wolfe was detained by Ellington security.

sixteen:

It was Saturday, and the countdown began for Halcyon and Sean to return to Atlanta. All of the family and friends were more than ready to see the Spencers. The ladies wanted to know about the sites and shopping, and the guys were ready to break in the basketball court at Spencer Manor.

Everyone was at the Chandler Mansion hanging out when Presscott got a call from an unfamiliar number. She answered her cell while she was standing in the kitchen. There was a sudden burst of laughter and she had to excuse herself to another room. When she was isolated she gave her undivided attention to the caller. "Hello this is Dr. Chandler, may I help you?" She asked.

"Yes ma'am Dr. Chandler ma'am. Mi nombre es Hector, I working you hermana casa. Something in basement mi no gusto. You vamanos aqui ahora, okay?" The gentleman stated with a thick Spanish accent.

"Comprendo. Can you tell me what's in the basement?" Presscott tried to inquire.

"Yes ma'am. Mi hermanos no working. Policia coming, vamanous aqui ahora."

Presscott was becoming very frustrated with the unknown, but when she heard the chirp of the police car the frustration instantly turned into panic. She then hung up the phone and walked over to Jonathan causally. She whispered in his ear and walked away with her hand rubbing across his chest. He pulled her back into an embrace and they kissed. When they stopped kissing he excused them both. Once they were clear of the kitchen she grabbed her purse and he grabbed a set of their car keys. They swiftly walked into the carriage house, he deactivated the car alarm and they both ran to the Lexus. Once they were safely in the car, Presscott briefed him again on what Hector said over the phone. The fifteen minute drive was in silence as they both wondered why the authorities had to be called to the mansion that had been inactive for two years.

When they pulled up to the mansion, police cruisers were everywhere and there was a body on a gurney. The face was not covered and an IV bag was lying on the person's chest. Presscott closed her eyes, took a deep breath and began to pray. Jonathan put his hand on top of her's and silently prayed as she prayed aloud.

A police officer then tapped on the driver side window. Jonathan leaned over and kissed her on the cheek, and then he opened the car door. Jonathan reached out his hand to the officer and said, "Good afternoon officer, my name is Jonathan Chandler and this is my wife Presscott.

"Hi, I'm Deputy Hines and from what I gathered here so far, your wife is the one these workers here called to the scene."

Jonathan wanted to laugh at the officer's thick southern drawl but he bit the inside of his mouth and refrained from doing so. Jonathan took a breath and stated, "Yes sir, my wife was the one that was called. Her sister does own the home, but we thought we should check this out first."

The deputy put a hand on one hip and said, "Well I dunno what you thought that for. It don't concern yall. It's not yalls propty."

Jonathan was about to respond when he heard his wife say, "Deputy Hines you are absolutely correct. My sister who owns this property suffered a great lost two years ago and we try to protect her heart from anything that may cause her distress."

"Umph," Deputy Hines didn't know how to respond, so he asked, "well folks can I git you to tell me who's on the gurney?"

Jonathan grabbed Presscott's hand followed the Deputy over to the gurney. As they got closer to the gurney Presscott became extremely weak as she realized who it was. Jonathan was still walking as her gait began to slow down and then came to a stop. Jonathan turned to his wife and asked, "Babe what's wrong?"

All the moisture in her mouth dried up as she whispered the question, "is that Anthony?"

Jonathan had his back to the gurney and he said to his wife, trying to console her, "Honey we buried Anthony a little over two years ago."

Presscott turned Jonathan towards the gurney and demanded, "Look at the guy on the gurney that is Anthony."

Jonathan began to protest and then stopped in mid-sentence as the gentleman on the gurney said, "Hey Jonathan, shocking huh? Is Hannah here?"

Anthony had beautiful locked hair that he kept shoulder's length and meticulously cleaned and conditioned but it was now unkempt and extremely dirty. He kept his feet and fingers manicured and now they were over grown and yellowed with jaundice. His hygiene was impeccable but he now carried a stench that was horribly out of this world. His eyes were a murky green color and clear, yet now they were cloudy and confused. His skin color was a deep olive and now he just looked dirty. He was extremely learned. His voice reminded you of James Earl Jones; deep and rich; now it was just above a whisper. He had Hannah's name tattooed on his left bicep.

Presscott stepped out from behind Jonathan as she began to remember things about Anthony. She walked up to the gurney cautiously. When she got close she just looked him over looking for a sign that it really was him. Then she said in a whisper, "May I see your left bicep?"

Jonathan just watched his wife as he tried to wrap his mind around what was happening.

Anthony pulled the sheet down so she could see the tattoo, it was there. Then he whispered something that only she could hear. That solidified it for her, she knew it was him. She kissed him on the cheek and whispered "welcome back" in his ear.

As Presscott lifted herself away from the gurney Anthony pleaded in a voice just above a whisper, "Scottie please don't let them take me to the family's hospital. All of this happened to me because of the family. Come to the hospital by yourself and I will tell you everything that happened."

As Anthony spoke she understood his plea and she decided to comply.

Immediately Presscott considered what was revealed at the last Railroad meeting. She turned around and surveyed the grounds on the property. Confusion was operating everywhere but everyone seemed to have a handle on everything except Jonathan. She had never seen her husband so discombobulated. Presscott made a mental note of how Jonathan seemed terrified to see Anthony alive. She began to walk toward him as he began to make a call on his cell phone.

She read his lips, "Sir, Anthony has been discovered."

Presscott immediately became alarmed and began to walk backwards towards the gurney wondering who he was speaking with. Was Jonathan a part of this?

When she reached the gurney she turned to the attending paramedic and asked, "Hello. May I ask you your name?"

"Yes ma'am. Lockett, Donovan Lockett," he answered her hurriedly.

"Mr. Lockett hi my name is Presscott Ellington, as in the Ellingtons," she began to explain.

Donovan gave her his full attention as he said, "Yes ma'am, I know who you are, the oldest of the four daughters and married to Jonathan Chandler."

Presscott looked down out of embarrassment because she was pulling rank on him and she was uncomfortable in doing so. "Yes sir that is me. I need you to pay close attention to me. What I am about to ask you to do is a matter of saving my brother-in-law's life."

Donovan looked her in her face anticipating her instructions, "I'm listening Dr. Chandler."

Presscott was impressed that he really knew who she was but she had no time to inquire. She looked over her shoulder at Jonathan and he was engrossed in the conversation on his phone, then she read his lips a second time, "He will be dead before I get back to the house."

She turned back to Donavan and said, "Okay Mr. Lockett. I need you to put my brother-in-law in the ambulance very quietly and drive him to Crawford Long Hospital with the siren off. I will be in the ambulance with him. We also need to unhook the low jack and the GPS and leave it right outside the front gate."

Donovan didn't ask any questions, he just began to move on her orders.

Anthony then asked, "Scottie what's happening?"

Presscott answered him by saying, "I am not sure Anthony but I can promise you that my sister is not going to have to bury you a second time any time soon."

Presscott saw Donovan slide under the ambulance and remove the low jack undetected. Then he and his partner slid Anthony into the back of the ambulance, along with Presscott stepping into the back as well. While Donovan drove his partner disarmed the GPS. The police road block allowed them to leave the property without checking to make sure they were clear to leave the property. When Donovan got to the edge of the Johnson's property he rolled down the window and threw the low jack and GPS out of the window.

As they drove to the hospital Presscott road in silence, she was trying to figure out what to do next. Then she leaned forward and asked Donovan to pull over at the next Quick Trip because she needed a disposable cell phone. She counted the cash in her pocket and handed Donovan three hundred dollars. She instructed him to get four disposable cell phones and to put twenty dollars on each phone. While Donovan was in Quick Trip, Presscott rested the back of her head against the wall of the ambulance, took a deep breath and let it out slowly. Then she leaned forward and looked Anthony straight in the eyes and asked him, "In short, what kind of threat do you pose to my family?"

Anthony liked how she presented the question. He knew she couldn't handle all of the details right now, he just simply said, "I know too much about how your dad runs his personal business."

Then Presscott remembered that her cell phone had a tracking device on it, so she quickly got the cell phone and turned it off, took the SIM card out and gave it to Donovan's partner to toss in the dumpster when they left the parking lot.

While the party was in full swing at the Chandler Mansion, Mudear made a special request of McKenzie privately. In a whisper in McKenzie's ear she asked, "Will you please meet me on the east porch in five minutes?"

McKenzie agreed because this was her opportunity to say some things to her mother that she had held in for some time and no one would be there to stop her. She responded with, "Yep." McKenzie didn't wait for five minutes, she made her way to the east porch right then. McKenzie paced on the porch until Mudear got there. When Mudear stepped onto the porch, McKenzie immediately asked, "What the hell is this little charade of yours about Elizabeth?"

Mudear took a step closer to McKenzie and asked, "Do you really know why you don't like me?"

McKenzie thought of several ways to answer that question, but she opted to take a step away from her mother instead. Mudear stepped closer because she if her daughter swung on her she did not want her to miss. Then she asked McKenzie, "Doesn't Presscott have a dance studio here?"

McKenzie felt her quick temper beginning to spark and she answered with a dry, "Yes."

Mudear turned to face McKenzie and then asked, "Would you dance for me there?"

McKenzie became cold, took a deep breath and answered, "No. I will not dance for you anywhere. What do you want with me?"

Mudear's eyes began to fill with tears and she said, "I need to set the record straight for you and your sisters, would you please set up another brunch for this week?"

McKenzie's cell phone began to vibrate, she looked down at the screen and saw Presscott's distress code with the railroad location. McKenzie began to walk away from Mudear but Mudear grabbed her hand and placed an oversized envelope in it.

Hannah looked around the Chandler mansion and noticed that both of her sisters were missing along with her mother. She couldn't believe that her sisters left her to entertain the guests by herself. She was trying to get an attitude about the situation when her cell phone began to vibrate. She removed the cell phone from her hip case and saw Presscott's distress code along with the railroad location. Extremely perplexed by the distress call she began to move quickly through the house making sure that her movements were not detected as she made her way to the carriage house. When she stepped into the secured section of the carriage house she noticed that all four of the identical Jaguars were still in place. As she looked at the cars she wondered what could possibly be wrong. Was the distress call a mistake?

"Hannah!" McKenzie yelled her name from behind her.

The yell startled Hannah and while she turned to face McKenzie she asked, "Do you have to be so loud and rude?"

"Hannah not now. Dismantle your tracking devise, dispose of it while you're in route, enter from the northeast and I will contact you in five minutes in your earpiece. Make sure it's secured in your ear and turned on."

Hannah hated when McKenzie acted like she was in charge whenever Presscott wasn't around.

seventeen:

Halcyon sat straight up in the bed for no apparent reason. She looked around the room as if some unknown entity were there but discovered nothing. She walked down to the kitchen, turned on the tea kettle and began to pace with great worry. She knew this had something to do with her sisters, she was very aware of that emotional ache in her heart. She picked up the cottage phone and tried to call all of her sisters and was unsuccessful in each attempt. She then found her cell phone and sent out a distress code to Presscott. No response. This was extremely out of character for Presscott. McKenzie was next on the list.

McKenzie and Hannah were talking to one another through their earpieces when McKenzie received a distress code from Halcyon. McKenzie's dash board was flashing the code and she said, "Han I'm getting a distress code from Cy, I'm going to patch her into our call." Hannah didn't respond; she just listened intensely.

Then she heard McKenzie say, "Hey Cy, it's me and Han on the line. Are you okay?"

Halcyon answered, "I'm okay but something is wrong there. What's going on? I can't reach Scottie."

McKenzie responded, "We don't know what's going on

but I'm going to keep you on the line so you will find out as we find out."

Halcyon didn't like the sound of that so she asked, "Kenny what are you not telling me? What are you not saying?"

McKenzie began to answer when she and Halcyon heard a soft and painful, "Oh God," from Hannah. Hannah pulled onto the gravel at the railroad first. She saw an ambulance. She got out of the car massaging her heart with her finger tips on her right hand. McKenzie pulled in right behind her and jumped out of her car.

McKenzie asked Hannah very gently, "What's wrong Han? You're massaging your heart."

Hannah stared at the ambulance as she answered, "Something is very wrong. My heart just synchronized with someone's. My heart only did that with one person and he died two years ago."

McKenzie didn't know what that meant, she was about to inquire when Presscott walked onto the gravel. Presscott's eyes locked with Hannah's and she took her by the hand.

Halcyon hung up her phone without saying goodbye. She went upstairs to the bedroom where Sean was sleeping. She woke him as gently as she could. She explained the conversation she just heard with her sisters she understood the synchronization of Hannah's heart.

Sean understood everything Halcyon said and then he began to explain everything he knew. Halcyon just wanted to be with her sisters and Sean complied.

Presscott didn't know how to explain to her sister that her husband was still alive. She was always the strong one of the four sisters and she had some extreme obstacles of her own that needed her immediate attention. So she did what came natural to her. She hugged both of her sisters at the same time with her head in between the both of theirs and said, "Anthony is alive."

Both sisters pulled away from her in disbelief. Hannah identified his body, she felt his cold lifeless clammy skin. McKenzie was at the funeral. She stared at him in the casket at the wake in disbelief. She helped comfort his mother at the repast.

Alive.

What?

Not possible.

Presscott just watched their reactions and she knew there was nothing else that she could say so she silently escorted them both into the railroad house. Hannah's grip became tighter in Presscott's hand and McKenzie freed her hand of Presscott's grip. Presscott didn't stop to acknowledge McKenzie's actions.

Standing outside McKenzie tried to wrap her head around the fact that Anthony was alive and when she heard Sean's name announced in her earpiece, she thought *now what?*

"Hey Sean." McKenzie answered.

"It's Cy Kennie." Halcyon's voice responded.

"I'm coming back home tonight but I will not be on an Ellington plane."

This was odd and McKenzie didn't' know how to process the information that Halcyon was saying to her. "Why?" McKenzie asked her sister.

"There are a lot of reasons why but the most important is that I miss my sisters and I need to be near all of you." Halcyon answered.

"Umph." McKenzie started her response then continued. "That's a nice thing to say Cy, but that's not why you are coming home. There is something major going on and you're not saying what it is."

"McKenzie."

"What?"

"What's wrong?"

"A lot."

"Are you going to tell me what's going on there?"

"Something tells me you already know."

"McKenzie."

"I have to go."

"McKenzie."

"Bye."

Disconnect.

McKenzie disconnected the phone call with a tap on the earpiece. She decided that she was not going into the railroad house. She loved her sisters so much but she honestly felt like the best thing for her right now was space. McKenzie decided now to focus all of her energy on her life. Her head was spinning trying to process how life as she knew it was coming to an end. It was a bitter sweet realization. McKenzie walked back to the Jaguar that she drove to the railroad. She sat in the car, disconnected the earpiece and picked up the envelope that Mudear put in her hand earlier.

eighteen:

Presscott found herself sitting in her closet. She was rummaging through everything without any particular goal in mind; she just needed to escape her reality. The shoes in her closet were now arranged by the inch of the heel and color. Outfits now coincided with the shoe. This is how Presscott wanted her life to be, she wanted everything in place, neat, clean and in order.

She then moved to the DVD cases in her closet. She alphabetized all of the DVD's and made sure they were in their appropriate cases. One DVD in particular caught her attention because it was unmarked, not in a case and very out of character for Presscott to have. She turned on the flat screen monitor. She grabbed the remote and pushed play. Jonathan's voice filled the space in the closet and then his face appeared on the flat screen.

"Scottie I need you to know how much I want to make this right. I hurt you bad, and I have to make this up to you. The only thing you required of me was honesty and I lied to you in a major way. Here's the truth, I love you. If my misery equates to your happiness, then miserable I will be. You tell me what you want from me and I will do exactly that. Please Scottie I only need you, I only want you and I only love you. Please Presscott don't leave me."

White noise then filled the space and Presscott held her hand to her chest tapping it trying to control her emotions. She turned the player off and tossed the remote on the chase lounge chair. Slowly she began to pace the length of the closet with her gaze held intently to the floor. Presscott's vision began to blur with tears as she scolded herself mentally not to cry. As she began to turn and walk away from the entrance of the closet, a hand slipped into hers and the journey to healing began.

Presscott assumed that McKenzie was walking with her, but it wasn't her younger sister. When they reached the chase lounge chair, Presscott was guided to sit down. Presscott didn't want to look up, because in her mind it was her mother consoling her and that could not happen.

The hands touched her face gently and the voice said, "Oldest daughter of mine. Daughter of mine we will make it through this."

This is a cruel joke, Presscott thought.

Mudear hugged Presscott and wouldn't let her go. Mudear whispered in Presscott's ear, "I apologize for all the pain that I caused you. I love you and I vow to protect you from this day forward. I love you baby."

Presscott tried to control the tears and deny the

aches in her heart. Controlling her emotions was the only defense that she had against the world and every time her mother would say, "I love you." her defense would crumble a little more. Then her gentle tears became uncontrollable sobs. Mudear held Presscott tight. Presscott eventually fell asleep to her mother humming an unknown lullaby, brushing the side of her face and a gentle rocking back and forth.

nineteen:

Hannah got Remminton to meet her at Moe's right around the corner from Crawford Long Hospital. Remmington walked into Moe's with her body guard, Paul. When Remmington saw Hannah she said, "Joe please tell me that we are not dining here."

Hannah could always count on her best friend to have a smart remark as a hello. Hannah stood to greet her friend as she escorted her out of the restaurant.

"Umm Joe, where are we going?" Remmington asked.

"If I tell you what we are up to you wouldn't believe me so I decided to show you." Hannah explained.

Remmington decided not to resist since her friend was solely responsible for her safety.

Hannah walked Remmington to the hospital. Remmington got excited because she thought maybe they were going to identify Corbin's dead body.

Hannah walked Remmington to a private room and opened the door. There Anthony lay in the bed. Remmington cocked her head to the side and squinted her eyes at the man in the bed. Remmington turned to Hannah and asked, "Who is this? Should I know him?"

"I thought you would always know me after I busted you at my wedding." The voice from the bed said.

Remmington locked eyes with Hannah with no prevalent emotion being displayed.

The voice said, "Remmy it's been a little over two years since you saw me last. My hair was locked. You love my wife dearly. We were going to plan a 'jus cuz' party for Hannah."

Remmington was scared to turn around so she just kept looking at Hannah. As Hannah watched Remmington she saw the realization set in that was indeed Anthony then Remmington asked Hannah, "I'm scared to look at him. Is it really my Anthony?"

Hannah smiled, "It's really him and he asked for you specifically."

This time when Remmington turned around and faced Anthony she covered her mouth and tried to blink away mixed emotions. She couldn't speak and as she walked over to the bed he sat up to give her a hug. They embraced and she squeezed him as tight as she could and he squeezed her back. She kept saying, "I love you," through tears. Once she composed herself she asked them how did this happen?

Anthony explained everything and while he was talking, Remmington started making the case connections. When Anthony finished talking, Remmington sat quietly for a moment and then she said, "I love you both but I gotta go talk to the B.A.U."

They said their goodbyes and Remmington was out the door.

Hannah walked over to the bed and laid in Anthony's arms. He kissed her on the forehead and asked, "What do you think Remmy is up to?"

"Well" she began, "Remmy has always been my best defense sense we were kids. There may be a connection between you, Kiki Combs and Cy, if anyone can figure this out its Remmington. When you started telling her about what happened to you she started seeing the missing pieces. She might have this solved by tonight."

Hannah didn't want to talk any more she just wanted to lay in her husband's arms. She wanted to smell him. She wanted to touch him. She wanted to hear him breath. She wanted to touch his face. She wanted to just look at him. She wanted this to be real. She got her baby back and life is wonderful again.

SECOND MEETING AT PRESSCOTT'S OFFICE

"Oh dear, it's my baby girl. How are you my love?" Presscott was so happy to see her baby sister. They embraced. Then Presscott led her sister to sit with her at the table, "I want to know everything you want to tell me." They were interrupted by the door opening and in walked McKenzie with Hannah and Lance in tow.

After the other sisters said hello to Halcyon, Halcyon turned to Lance with an outstretched hand and said, "Hello I'm Cy, the youngest Ellington."

"Hey beautiful lady, you are simply gorgeous."

"Thank you."

"No, thank you for being so beautiful. My name is Lance."

"Lance, the New York realtor?"

"Yes baby in the flesh...all day long."

"Huh."

"Well Cy," McKenzie interrupted, "Lance is here because apparently Michael and Shauna have been set up in a sex scandal."

"So where are we starting?" Halcyon asked.

For hours they sat in the conference room piecing events, conversations and the surveillance feed together.

Halcyon then asked, "Can you think of anyone who would want to sabotage you like this?"

"No and the one I want to blame is proving to be an innocent." McKenzie responded.

Halcyon just smiled because she knew her sister was referring to their mother. Once they were happy with the accuracy of the time line they adjourned.

TEXT MESSAGE:

8:30 Breakfast at Chandler man. Scottie

CC: Ken, Han, Cy, Rem

REPLY:

Can we change ven to Ritz? Han

REPLY:

k. Scottie

REPLY:

k. Cy

REPLY:

k. Rem

REPLY:

k. The Ken

NEXT MORNING

8:15 on the dot Presscott was knocking on Hannah's suite door. The door was opened immediately and Presscott was greeted by all invited attendees in their pajamas. She was dressed in jeans and a button down shirt, she felt overdressed.

"Good morning Oldest. Here are some PJ's for you." Halcyon greeted Presscott and then continued with, "Isn't it nice not to have to wait for anyone?"

"Yes. I have missed you something terrible baby girl." Presscott smiled at her sister and then slipped into the

PJ's.

"I missed you more Doc and please don't try to convince yourself of something different." Halcyon said standing right outside the doorway of the bathroom.

"No argument here. I promise newlywed." Presscott said while she touched Halcyon's nose with the inside of her bent index finger.

Halcyon then whispered, "Scottie you were right."

Presscott whispered back with a perplexed look on her face, "About what?"

Halcyon blushed.

Then Presscott whispered again with a smile, "We'll talk later."

"Okay you two," McKenzie began to yell, "it's 8:30 we have a lot of ground to cover."

Hannah had five of every breakfast item that was on the menu delivered to her suite. Hannah pulled out about four pieces of paper and began with, "Halcyon I don't know what all you already know about what's been happening. So please feel free to interject for clarification on anything. The floor is open to everyone for clarification. Now we are going to go through the time line that was created last night point by point. I want to start with the name Corbin Wolfe."

Remmington swallowed hard as McKenzie asked, "Who the hell is Corbin Wolfe?"

Hannah explained that the first time that she heard his name pertaining to the family issue was through Mudear two nights before the brunch.

"Really?" Remmington asked.

"Really." Hannah answered.

"Why?" Remmington asked.

"She wanted me to consider going out with him." Hannah explained.

"Joe I am so sorry." Remmington apologized.

"No love lost I promise. Now it is making sense to me." Hannah responded.

"Okay," McKenzie interrupted, "you two heffas want to share the secret?"

"I apologize." Hannah said and then continued with, "This will make sense in a moment. Now Cy have you heard about the brunch?"

"Only what was discussed last night." Halcyon said very innocently.

Tension immediately took a bold seat amongst the ladies.

Presscott cleared her throat and said, "I will take this one." Presscott only touched on the highlights. Halcyon scribbled some notes when Presscott mentioned the rape.

Hannah spoke up and asked Halcyon how she was doing.

Halcyon was the stone wall of the sisters; you could never read what she was feeling. She gently encouraged Hannah to continue with a simple nod.

McKenzie then explained the affair, the pregnancy, the break-up and then the abortion. The purpose of Lance was explained. Now last night made perfect sense to her.

Halcyon got up and walked over to McKenzie and said, "I am forever for you and this matter is priority to me. I don't care what I discover; I am not going to stop until I reach the end." Then Halcyon got real close to McKenzie's ear and whisper, "watch Lance." She then kissed her on the top of her head and sat back down. "What's next?" Halcyon asked as she cleared her throat.

Neither sister responded outwardly to the whisper.

Hannah now explained the importance of Corbin Wolfe starting with a question, "Cy does the name Corbin Wolfe sound familiar to you?"

"No. Should it?" Halcyon asked.

"He went to Dunwoody Prep with you and you both did your undergrad together." Hannah stated.

Halcyon then said as she stared into space, "My freshmen year of undergrad I met Sean so I truly cannot recall any special guys from college. The only guy I remember from Dunwoody Prep is Jenkins."

"Jenkins huh..." Remmington started, "what do you remember about him?"

"Well, he was the star point guard for the basketball team. He was incredibly fine. He asked me to prom and I declined because Amanda Winston told me I better not go with him." Halcyon smiled at the long lost memory.

Remmington then explained the Kiki Combs case and the potential Halcyon connection.

"Okay, okay, okay..." McKenzie chirped in, "I need about a thirty minute recess damn it."

They all agreed.

THIRTY MINUTES LATER

"Well ladies..." Remmington started when everyone settled, "I may have the answer to the Corbin Wolfe mystery."

"Okay, prey tale." Hannah responded for everyone.

Remmington then explained that Mudear's assailant's name was Dexter Edward Jenkins, he was a basketball star in high school and in college. He eventually became the last owner of the Atlanta Hawks. Currently he has the been officially missing for the past twenty four years, therefor declared legally dead. "Corbin Wolfe" legally changed his name five years ago from Dexter Edward Jenkins, Jr."

"So..." Presscott began, "what we now know is Sr. raped Mudear and he could be my father. Sr. is missing and now Jr. is coming after Cy. Is that it in a nutshell?"

"Yes." Remmington answered.

The room fell to an uneasy silence. Then Remmington continued, "Detective Brendel will be here in twenty minutes to take me to the B.A.U. to see if I can help feel in some blanks."

"Why you?" McKenzie asked through frustration.

"Because... I slept with him."

No one said a word. The explanation just hung in the air organically.

Remmington went into the adjoining room to change clothes.

McKenzie broke the silence with, "I don't get it, why him?'

"You have never seen him obviously." Hannah said.

"He can't be all that." McKenzie stated.

Halcyon blushed. Hannah took a deep breath and cleared her throat. Presscott pulled his picture up on her laptop and let out a quiet, "Ooooooo..."

Presscott turned the laptop toward McKenzie and her immediate response was, "Oh my damn! Shiiiiiiit!"

McKenzie then tried to turn the laptop towards Halcyon, she studied the picture for a moment and said, "Nothing has changed, that is Dexter Jenkins. I should have taken the beating and went to prom with him "

They all laughed and Hannah passed the laptop back to Presscott without looking at it, then Hannah said, "Okay re-focus."

"I understand why Remmy got hooked and fileted. Hey! IJS!" McKenzie said and ended with, "Okay yall I'm bringing it back, I'm bringing it back. Lord that was some kind of fine, mmm." Then she raised her hand like she was agreeing with a Preacher's words in church.

"Hooked and fileted?" Presscott repeated in a question then laughed.

Halcyon laid her head in her left hand and just laughed.

"If I would have met him first, I would have fileted the Tilapia, breaded it and did a slow cooked it for him without him asking."

Everyone turned and looked at innocent Hannah in shock.

Then she said, "IJS."

"No she didn't." McKenzie said.

"Wow..." Halcyon said with amazement.

"Well I think we can conclude that Kennie has finally rubbed off on Han." Presscott said.

They all just laughed and started bringing up old fun memories from childhood. No one noticed that Remmington walked out of the suite.

twenty:

Presscott was listening to the local live band in the backyard playing One Note Samba. She was really appreciating the vocalist who was fusing the Nancy Wilson and Ella Fitzgerald versions of the song. Brilliant.

Then Halcyon grabbed Presscott's hand and led her to the dance floor. The song had changed to Tania Maria's Agua de Beber, and the sisters danced together. In the middle of the song Halcyon pulled Presscott into an embrace and whispered in her ear, "Sean is flying me to Texas tonight."

Presscott squeezed her sister tight and whispered back, "I understand but Cy I just got you back."

"You can come out whenever you want okay."

"Okay. How long will you be there?"

"Until all concerns are dealt with here completely. Sean started working on something about two months before we got married."

Presscott looked perplexed.

The other sisters joined in the dance and the four of them danced until dawn, literally.

Before the sisters separated to retire early that morning, Presscott asked them, "Are you all aware that I can read lips fluently?"

Halcyon and Hannah said, "No," in unison.

McKenzie turned Presscott's head to her and mouthed, "Bitch please, prove it."

Presscott laughed with a response out loud, "This is the first and last time you will ever get away with calling me bitch. Please do not make me prove anything to you."

They all laughed and then Presscott continued with, "When Stanley saw you and Sean, he made a call to ambush the both of you. I do not know who he was talking to." All four of the sisters were uneasy then Presscott turned to McKenzie and said, "Stanley is also going after Michael and Lance."

McKenzie became upset asking, "Why?"

"I don't know Younger, but I need you to stay focused."

Then she took a deep breath and continued with, "We all need to stay focused because we do know that killing family is not a big deal for Stanley. By the way, I'm not sure how this is connected but those two plane crashes we heard reported on last night have been cleaned up. You won't hear another report on them. As of right now, none of us are safe in an Ellington plane."

Presscott ended with this, "Han let's keep Anthony's return amongst us as long as possible."

They all said their goodbyes and hugged one another.

Presscott did not know what to do next except get away and think things through with no distractions.

ILSE OF MANN

There under the weeping willow tree Presscott laid trying to figure out what to do with her life next. She went to the doctor and found out that was six weeks pregnant. She does not want to co-parent her child but she sincerely believed that was the route she may have to take. So she laid there with Lizz Wright playing in the background at her quaint little cottage that she built for herself in the British Isle of Mann. No one would find her here; this was her own private place.

She finally came to grips with it was time to tell her sisters everything that she did not say when they all met at the Ritz. The news about Jonathan's involvement with Anthony is going to crush them. She could not figure out how to protect her sisters from certain truths and that was one of Presscott's biggest concerns and now she was pregnant. She strongly considered never returning, but she knew it would only be a matter of time before McKenzie invaded her space very loudly. So she boarded a plane the next afternoon.

Presscott decided to just be in her home unannounced, alone. She lay across her bed and

Jonathan's absence was felt strongly and she longed to breathe him in deeply but that truly was not the answer or an option. She knew she would have to have a conversation with him that would certainly tear her world apart. She wanted to know why when she read his lips she comprehended what she did. Presscott hated him and loved him in the same moments. Surely there was a logical explanation. She wanted to know; she wanted him to make her understand. She wanted him to reassure her that all of this was a simple innocent misunderstanding. She longed to have her life back.

Presscott was so into her thoughts as she lay on the bed that she did not hear her bedroom door open. She felt a presence in the room with her but she did not wonder who it was. If someone had broken in to do her harm, she did not care. She wanted someone, anyone to stop her heart from feeling all together. She felt a pair of lips kiss her on the cheek and she automatically knew it was Jonathan. He would not stop her heart from hurting; he was going to cause more pain.

"I love you." He whispered in her ear.

Presscott did not respond to him verbally. She rolled away from him so her back was to him.

"Can I talk to you?" he asked.

She closed her eyes, swallowed hard and still did not

respond verbally. He touched her arm gently and sent an unexpected amazing chill up her spine. A moan of pleasure escaped from her throat without permission. A single tear made a path across the bridge of her nose.

Presscott began with, "I read your lips at the Johnson mansion." She paused for him to say something but he did not. "I believe I read, 'Sir, he will be dead before I leave the property.' Am I right?"

Jonathan could not think fast enough. He did not want his wife psycho analyzing him about anything, because now he felt completely raw and naked before her; even with her back turned towards him. He finally answered with his eyes closed, "Yes."

Nothing was said between them for about thirty seconds.

Then Presscott said," Jonathan can you explain that?"

"Honey can we talk about it later?" he asked her.

"No, we cannot." she answered him very flatly.

"Why not?" He asked knowing he was trying to buy some time to think of an answer.

"You came to me and asked me to talk." She said starting to get agitated.

Jonathan reached over her and turned on the light next to the bed. He noticed her tears and grabbed a tissue and began to wipe them away. "What are these about?" he asked in a whisper.

She cleared her throat and said, "Please don't." She pushed his hand away before she continued, "These tears are about the fact that it pains me to think that my husband is a hit man. How do I explain this to our child? These tears are also about how bad I want to fall slave to your touch but my head, my logic won't allow me. I wanted to tell you about our pregnancy during a very erotic sex session." Her voice broke as she continued with a soft staccato emphasis on, "I don't know who I married."

It was worse than Jonathan thought. She did not raise her voice. She rolled over on her back and looked him in his eyes.

He was not going to lie to her, he just did not know how much of the truth to tell.

"Are you willing to allow me to ask you any questions and you answer them truthfully?" Presscott asked him trying to make the conversation easier for him.

"Yes." he said while he grabbed her hand and placed it on his heart.

Presscott knew this was going to be hard but she proceeded with her eyes closed. "Who were you talking to on the phone?"

Jonathan's heart began to pound in his chest, he felt this was going to be real bad, but he promised himself to be honest. He took a deep breath and said, "Your dad."

She could not have heard him right. She sat up in the bed and turned her body so she was face to face with him, she put her hand back on his heart and asked, "My who?"

"Your dad."

"Who was the hit for?"

"Anthony."

Presscott slowly pulled her hand off of Jonathan's heart. She was no longer crying. She could not understand what she was feeling for him, if anything at all. This was not the Jonathan Kevin Chandler, IV that she fell in love with and married. He was always the first to comfort Hannah when she was missing Anthony. Jonathan went with Hannah and Presscott to identify Anthony's body.

Presscott turned on the bed to get up and Jonathan grabbed her.

She was scared.

"I'm pregnant." It was a shameful ploy in an attempt to protect oneself; she had never been afraid of him before.

He noticed the look in her eyes. He began to plead

with her, "Please don't be afraid of me. I would never hurt you. I love you. Scottie please don't be afraid of me."

She didn't want to be afraid of him. He just admitted that he was going to kill her supposedly dead brother-in-law. She needed to get away from him and now. "Jonathan please let me go." her voice began to waiver.

"What can I do to make this go away? Tell me how to make this right. Honey I want us back. I need to be a husband to you and a daddy to our child." Now he was really pleading and she was begging through tears for him to let her go. He finally let her go and she walked swiftly to her closet. She did not close the door. She changed into a loose fitting jogging suit and some matching tennis shoes. When she walked out of the closet and Jonathan saw her, he stood up and blocked the door.

"Where are you going Scottie? It's late." He said.

"I don't know." She answered with her head down.

"I can't let you leave like this." He gently raised her chin up.

"What do you mean?" She asked diverting her eyes anywhere other than his face.

"I don't want you to be afraid of me." He said deflated.

"I don't want to be afraid of you," she said catching her breath.

Jonathan looked away from her for a moment and in that moment she bolted out of the bedroom. She knew if he chased her, he would catch her but she was not going to make it easy for him. When she reached the top of the stairs, she heard his footsteps close behind her. She faked right as if she were going to run down the stairs. He anticipated the move and tried to beat her to the stairs. She ducked below his out stretched arm and jumped up on the banister rail. She took two steps on the rail and catapulted herself into the long hallway. This move put distance between her and Jonathan. She ran straight for the room at the end of the hallway. Presscott slammed and locked the door in one movement. She quickly went to the closet and closed the door. This closet was an elevator. She pushed "G" for garage and prayed that Jonathan forgot about that particular elevator in the house. When she got off the elevator there he stood waiting. She was no longer afraid, she was angry. He escorted her to the great room on the first floor in silence. She sat at the massive dining table and he sat across from her.

He stared at her. "Why did you run and when did you learn to run across banisters?" He asked her.

"It's called survival instincts and I free run twice a week." She answered not breaking her stare with him.

"Scottie why? You don't have to be a..."

She cut his words off.

"You just admitted to me that you were going to kill Anthony!" She shocked herself with the sound of her voice. That was the one thing that Presscott did not do, she did not raise her voice.

Jonathan was shocked.

"You said you don't want me to be afraid of you and I am desperately trying not to be." Presscott's voice was calm and steady again.

"This is all just a misunderstanding and I need to figure out how to tell you the truth." The back of Jonathan's neck was starting to get warm.

"I am your wife, you don't figure out what is true with me, truth just is." Presscott stated as if she were in a counseling session.

"Honey I have to be careful with how I share certain things with you." Jonathan was really trying to get a lie together.

Presscott squinted her eyes as Jonathan spoke to her.

"Why are you looking at me like that?" Jonathan asked.

"Because you are lying and it really hurts to see that

is what you have deduced our relationship to. Jonathan when I took my marriage vows I truly meant them when I took them. For some reason I know this is something we can work through. I have always had one condition and I told you that condition when we first started dating. Truth." she said as she placed her elbows on the table and rested her head in her hands.

"I'm so sorry honey. This was not supposed to happen. You should not have to know any of this."

Presscott's thoughts started spinning as she tried to grasp what Jonathan was saying. "Jonathan I don't think we are going to solve anything tonight. You are going to keep dancing around the few facts that I know. Your two worlds have finally collided and I'm caught in the middle of the collision. I don't like this at all." She took a breath and continued, "I loved you with everything. I relied on you. I would have given up everything to be with you. I never cared about what we had or didn't have, I just wanted to breath you every chance I got. I always felt completely protected when you were around. Now I just don't feel the same about you. So no, we don't have to talk tonight. I will let you decide when we talk. Right now, my heart is aching and I don't want to sit here with you anymore. I'm leaving this house and please don't follow me."

Jonathan was not prepared for that last part. Where would she go at one thirty in the morning? "Presscott here, I will leave you stay okay?" he asked her sincerely.

Presscott stood up and just looked at him for a moment through tears then said, "You are my heart's ache and this house represents you. I no longer want to be here."

Jonathan felt his throat began to constrict and his palms began to get clammy. "Presscott please will you wait until later today, you need your rest. I don't want you out now."

Then she thought, *is something already in the works for her if she left this house tonight? He wouldn't do that would he? Well let's see.* "Good night Jonathan." She said with no emotion and moved around the table to leave.

Jonathan stood in her way for the second time that night.

He put her face in his hands and kissed her lips while whispering repeatedly, "I love you."

Presscott fought hard not to return the kisses. She wanted her life back. She remembered when they first moved into this mansion. The furniture would not be delivered until the following day. They built a fort with the extra blankets and pillows they found in the guest room. They found a little food in the main kitchen along with a bottle of White Zinfandel. They had to snuggle tight because the great room was cold. They told one another funny stories about their childhoods. Then they talked about when they knew they would be together forever. It was a beautiful night that they shared together. Now here is the end of the Chandlers in the same room that it officially began.

Presscott looked into Jonathan's eyes and tried to figure out if this was the last time that she would see him. She loved him so much. She allowed her lips to reach up to his. She kissed him without embracing him. It was a long kiss and without realizing it she began to cry yet again. Jonathan's world always collapsed when she cried but this time his world crumbled into a million pieces because he was the source of her tears.

She stepped out of the kiss.

He would not turn his gaze away from her eyes.

She walked to the front door. Now sobbing she said, "I love you so much."

He pleaded with her not to go.

She placed her hand on the door knob.

His voice became louder with his plea for her to stay in the house.

She opened the door. He jumped in front of her.

There was no sound.

She watched Jonathan fall to the floor in slow motion with a thud.

Presscott slammed the door shut and tried to help Jonathan move. He did not move. She noticed his eyes fluttering. She got down on her knees and leaned in close to Jonathan and began to call his name softly. Jonathan's eyes squeezed tight and then he coughed.

Presscott just watched him with no expression at all on her face. He grabbed her arm and pulled her closer to him because he had something important to tell her.

"Go to 'G'...my truck... file under seat... I love you... move now! move now..."

Presscott rolled away from him and hid in a cabinet so she could see the front door. The front door was kicked in. Jonathan was shot in the head twice execution style. Presscott suppressed her screams with the palm of her hand as five executioners searched her house.

Then she heard: *Sir Mrs. Chandler is still alive, Mr. Chandler took the kill shot.* Silence.

We are in the home searching for her now. Silence.

Yes Sir, I understand she is to be executed on site. I will call you with a report in an hour.

Fear gripped everything within her and then the door to the cabinet opened where she was hiding. The guy that was on the phone pulled her out of the cabinet and said to her in a very forcefully whisper, "I never saw you. You have one hour to disappear."

"But my husband sir," Presscott wanted to stay with her husband.

The gentleman repeated himself in the same demanding whisper, "You have one hour to disappear."

"Please let me stay with my husband?" Presscott was begging.

The gentleman pulled his gun from his holster and pointed it to her face.

Presscott stepped into the gun without flinching.

The gentleman then re-aimed the gun at her stomach.

Presscott then said through anger, "Not fair." She hesitated and then immediately made her way to the secret elevator and activated 'G' on the panel, she wanted to at least say goodbye to her husband; she loved him. She went to Jonathan's truck and found the file. There was a note on the outside of the file that read: The suburban is bullet proof GET OUT NOW!

She understood. She drove to Quick Trip and bought the biggest bag of sunflower seeds she could find and six 16oz bottles of Cherry Coke. When she returned to the vehicle she then put Nonny's address in the GPS and left Atlanta undetected.

twenty-one:

McKenzie was in New York trying to piece her life back together. She decided to deal with the most difficult thing first, Michael and the abortion. So she called him.

The phone rang three times before it was answered, "Hello." Michael answered.

"Hey, how are you?" McKenzie asked in her sweet sing songy kind of voice.

"McKenzie?" Michael asked.

"Yes it's me." McKenzie answered.

"Why are you calling me?" He asked through irritation.

"I thought we needed to talk, maybe I'm wrong." Now she was getting irritated.

"Your father made it clear that I am to never talk to his precious McKenzie again." He began to raise his voice in anger.

"What are you talking about? This is between you and me." McKenzie was biting the inside of her mouth trying to mask her anger.

"Well your father doesn't think so."

Disconnect.

McKenzie was livid. She then yelled, "Sammy!" With stiff arms and closed fists.

Sammy just appeared in the doorway without saying a word.

She turned toward the window and began to fuss, "I don't know who he thinks he is, hanging up on me. I still love this stupid mutha. I'm trying to make things right and then he's gonna put my father in it, Sammy!" She yelled his name again at the top of her lungs.

"I'm right here." He said very calmly.

The sound of his voice startled her, then she said, "Find the boy dancer and get him to Coopper's Tavern in twenty minutes."

"McKenzie, have a seat." Sammy said as a soft demand.

"Why I gotta have a seat? I need to talk to the boy dancer." She said protesting as she sat behind her desk.

"Before you go and talk to the 'boy dancer' you need to know some unpleasant things about your father."

McKenzie didn't know what to say except, "Okay."

"While you were in Atlanta I began my own investigation of you and Michael." He began.

McKenzie gave Sammy her full attention, she did not interrupt.

"Your father has something called the Son-In-Law Contract. The 'boy dancer', as you refer to him, would have never gotten your father's blessings for marriage because of his financial status. He can't contend with Ellington money. When your father found out Michael's net worth, he decided to break you two up with the body doubles. When you went to Nova Scotia and found out you were pregnant, the doctor reported that directly to S.P.E. or your father." Sammy stopped talking to let her process what he just said to her.

"Is there more?" She asked.

"Yes, but it goes downhill on a steep slope." He answered.

"Okay, tell me the rest of this shit." She was really trying to control her temper.

"When S.P.E. found out you were pregnant, he went after Michael himself. Michael was returning on a train from South Carolina. Your father got on that train, told Michael you were pregnant and if he did not break things off with you for good you would be killed in his arms at the airport.

"What the fu, you lying, You Lying, YOU LYING!" She was really trying to stay calm as she shook her head back and forth. She stood up very forcefully and began to pace back and forth. Then she said, "Go ahead witcha lil story."

Sammy cleared his throat and pulled out a picture.

The picture was of her and Michael on the tarmac when she announced the pregnancy to him. There were two red dots on her back and one on the back of her head.

She looked at Sammy and then back at the picture and said, "What is this?"

"Two to the body and one to the head, this is how we are trained to kill people. Two shots to cripple, one shot to the head to kill." He answered with no emotion. "I don't know what all your family is wrapped up in but this job, I no longer want. Everything in me is telling me to get out. I will stay on until I am sure you are safe and then I will find my replacement."

"Really? Wow..."

"McKenzie I can't stand by and watch your dad kill people just because..."

A siren sound alerted Sammy that there was an S.P.E. emergency. He read the message and then looked at McKenzie with extreme tension in his face.

"What's wrong?" McKenzie cautiously asked.

"Your brother-in-law, Jonathan, was killed last night. The bullets were for Presscott. Now I'm supposed to help find her so she can be eliminated. Come with me, the plan to keep you safe has just been activated."

McKenzie's head was spinning as she stood up to follow Sammy. Then she heard Sammy say activating his earpiece, "7.5 to Spencer, 4.5 to underground."

She did not know what that meant.

Hannah, Remmington and Anthony decided to have dinner at Dante's Down the Hatch at Five Points, they took the train in because they were trying to feel normal again.

In the middle of dinner and light conversation Hannah asked Anthony, "What is the 'Son-In-Law' contract?"

"Well it's a contract that your father insisted that if any man wanting to marry one of his daughters, they had to agree and sign." Anthony simply stated.

"What are the conditions?" Remmington asked nonchalantly.

Anthony laughed and then he said, "The daughters are not supposed to know about it."

"Shut up," Remmington said playfully.

"Seriously." Anthony said.

"Why are we not allowed to know about it?" Hannah asked.

"Because of what you two are doing right now." He said.

Hannah and Remmington looked at each other inquisitively.

"You see you just don't tell any of the Ellington

daughters anything without at least one of them inspecting the validity; I actually think that is a great quality. Your father never wanted you girls to know about how he intended for the Ellingtons to always stay on top." Anthony began to explain.

"What do you mean?" Hannah asked.

"I'm only going to explain what happened to me." He grabbed Hannah's hand and cleared his throat before he continued. "According to the contract I had to prove that I could deposit a million dollars into an 'Ellington' account that only your father controlled. If my financial status could support that condition then he would give his blessing for the marriage."

"But Anthony your name alone pulls in about ten million alone annually." Remmington said it like it was common knowledge.

Anthony looked at Hannah with a question on his face.

Hannah threw her hands up in surrender and said, "I have never discussed your financial status with Remmy or anyone."

"Then you fell in love and married an Ellington...your financial status went from millions to just O's." Remmington said and they all laughed.

"Anyway," Anthony began again, "So I had the

blessing but I still would not sign because the contract states that our first male child had to be an Ellington. In the event of a divorce I would lose all parental rights to my son. With the divorce, I would have to resign fifty-seven percent of my value over to your father. I would have to become a silent investor in all of his ventures. In the event that I did not sign, the wedding would be stopped and or I could lose my life."

"Babe..." Hannah was cut off by Anthony.

"I definitely wasn't signing and I opted to get whatever time I could get with you, whether it was seconds or years."

"Mmmm...I love you so much Anthony." Remmington said.

Anthony and Hannah looked at Remmington and at the same time said, "We love you too Remmy."

Hannah leaned back in her seat and weighed everything that Anthony just explained while he and Remmington talked more about the contract.

Then Hannah began to ask, "So does this mean Jonathan..."

Anthony cut her off by answering, "signed the contract? Yes."

Hannah sat there for a moment taking it all in, then she said, "Remmy find the most recent copy of the contract and find the loop hole."

"Babe wait," Anthony did not want to hurt her but he decided the truth was the best, "Jonathan was the ring leader for my death, that's why I'm not dead. When I was discovered alive he had to promise my death and he did not deliver. Sean and Cy are in hiding right now because of the contract. Michael never came close to the first financial status so that is why McKenzie and Michael are not a couple."

"Anthony I'm so sorry we fell in love." Hannah was so deflated.

"I'm not. I am getting to spend two life times with the woman I love the most." Anthony declared.

"Check this out Ant," Remmington said, "This right here will cause you to win every argument you guys have from here on out." Remmington was laughing.

"What?" Hannah asked.

"Every time you say no to him all he has to say is, 'but baby your daddy killed me.'" They all laughed.

Then Hannah noticed her body guard, Eddie Post walking toward the table with purpose. When he got within ear shot of Hannah, she asked, "Postman what's wrong?

"I need the three of you to follow me right now. I will explain in the car." He then reached into his pocket and put all of his bills on the table.

They got into a black suburban with the windows tinted extremely dark. As they got settled into the truck they heard guns clicking and then aimed outward behind the windows.

The truck began to move.

"Post what's up?" Anthony asked.

Eddie faced the front of the truck with his hand on his gun, clicking the safety off.

"Let me know when we are safely on Peachtree and make sure you obey ALL the traffic laws." Post said to the driver.

"Yes sir." The driver responded.

The truck was quiet for a beat and then the driver said, "Sir we are now moving safely through the traffic on Peachtree."

Post then activated his earpiece and said, "Sir code red has successfully been activated and all of my eggs are nestled safely in the nest. ETA thirty mics." Then Post turned his attention to the occupants of the truck, "Sorry for extracting you guys like that but those were my orders."

No one said anything.

Then Post continued, "Jonathan your brother-in-law was killed last night." All of the air in the truck evaporated.

"Not this shit again." Anthony said very angrily.

Post continued with, "The order was for the execution of Presscott."

All three of them said, "Who?"

"Presscott," Post repeated, and then he continued with "now I am supposed to help locate her so she can be executed."

"So what are we doing now? If you are using us to get to Scottie, my advice to you is to kill me before I kill you. This shit stops right here." Anthony said as he took his seatbelt off.

"Anthony, Hannah and Remmington please understand that I am on the daughters' side. As of right now I know for sure that Presscott is safe and I know her location." Post had to reassure them all.

Presscott sat in the drive way of Nonny's house reading the file Jonathan left under the seat. She did not know what to make of this. Would she ever know the truth? She owns her own business that could definitely take care of her and her unborn child. She knew she would always had her sisters and she needed to reach her mother. They had a much needed moment in her closet and right now she wanted her mother.

The knock on the window startled her. The realization of who was knocking pissed her off.

Presscott rolled down the window and said, "If you are going to keep showing up in my life uninvited please kill me, I beg of you."

"In order to keep you alive, I need you to come with me now." He said.

"Sir, I don't want to live so you can leave." Presscott said very confidently with her decision.

"You picked up a personal passenger about six weeks ago, they might want you to re-think that decision." He said as a rebuttal to her request.

"How did you know that?" She asked.

"It's my job to know everything about you. Let's go." He said.

"I'm not going anywhere with you," she said.

"It wasn't a question." He responded and then continued with, "and I'm not starting a debate." He reached into the truck's window and placed a cloth over her nose. Presscott passed out within moments. He then reached into the truck and very carefully removed her from one truck and placed her into another. He noticed the Cherry Cokes in the truck and took them along with the file she was reading. Then he activated his earpiece and said, "I got her. ETA eight hours."

"Have you heard from any of the children?" Mudear asked Mr. Ellington as they sat at the dining room table with breakfast being served.

"No, but after your brunch stunt do you really think they would be running to your side?" He asked.

"Okay Stanley not today." Mudear stood up to leave.

"Elizabeth, sit down." He demanded through clenched teeth.

"Not today Stanley." She repeated herself and kept walking out of the dining room.

He grabbed her by the back of her head and pulled her back into the dining room very forcefully.

Then one of the male servants snatched Mudear out of his arms and sat her in one of the seats at the table. Mr. Ellington began the fight with the male servant but he was no match for him.

When the fight ended, the male servant turned to Mudear and said, "Ma'am are you okay?"

"Yes, thank you." She answered in disbelief.

"Ma'am come with me we have to move quickly." He said.

She did not respond verbally, she just started moving.

Then she heard him say, "She's safe. ETA thirty

mics."

Halcyon had a lot of nervous energy as she tried to make herself busy around the house. She re-arranged the furniture in all of the guest bedrooms. She became an extreme couponer so she re-arranged her stock pile house every day. She fussed at herself often for agreeing to allow Sean to deal with the Ellington situation. She could not believe how messy her family was, her father in particular and she could not believe that Sean had not asked for a divorce yet.

"Cy, are you in here?" Sean was looking for her.

"Back here." She yelled out.

She could hear his footsteps and she became concerned because he was walking towards her with great purpose. She began walking towards him and when they met up she asked, "What's wrong?"

"Nothing. It's time to go to Smyrna." He said with a smile.

"Really? So everyone is okay?" She asked.

"Yes, but Michael and Presscott had to be kidnapped." He answered.

"Are you serious?" She asked.

"I'm sure the stories are amusing." He started and then continued with, "Let's go catch a plane."

She then pulled Sean close to her and kissed him very passionately and then said, "Thank you."

"You are very welcomed," he said as he kissed her back and then he asked, "Do you want to make it up to me?"

She was not sure what Sean was thinking, so she asked cautiously, "What do you have in mind Sir?"

"You have to fly naked," he said hoping for a yes.

"Only if we eventually cause our own turbulence," she answered.

"Ooo you nasty," he said with a smile.

"I will create some new nasty if you let me ride first," she said trying to be seductive.

"Ooo I'm telling on you," he said playfully.

While Sean was talking, Halcyon started running to the car yelling, "First one to the car rides first."

Halcyon beat Sean to the car. She told the driver that they needed some time. When Sean got in the car she was naked from the waist down.

"Cy what are you doing?" He asked almost embarrassed.

"I never said where the riding would begin," she said with a naughty smile on her face.

Sean and Halcyon Spencer were definitely newlyweds.

twenty-two:

Halcyon walked into the underground compound and was thoroughly impressed. She immediately wanted to see the blueprints so she could locate her sisters' quarters. She wanted to see them, she needed to see them. As Halcyon studied the sibling living quarters she noticed some names that were unfamiliar to her.

"Sean, who are these people in the sibling quarters? I don't know these names." She pointed to the names of Nikko, Juan and Nina.

"Let's find Scottie and figure this out." He led her to a golf cart and activated Presscott's coordinates.

"You know who they are, don't you?" Halcyon asked Sean.

"Yes." He answered as they drove to Presscott's quarters.

"Will you tell me who they are?"

"No."

"Why?"

"It's not for me to tell."

"But Sean I want to know."

"You my love will find out with everyone else."

"Sean Patrick!"

"Halcyon Joy is such a pretty name."

"Don't mock me."

"We're here...let's go."

Halcyon got out of the golf cart, turned towards Sean and said, "This isn't over."

"Yes it is. I love you and Scottie is in there." He said very easy.

Halcyon walked into the suite to find Presscott being examined by a doctor. Presscott turned towards the sound of the door and immediately smiled when she saw her baby sister.

"Everything is fine. You are officially cleared for anything NOT strenuous." The doctor said with a smile.

"Yes ma'am. Thank you for everything." Presscott said very sweetly and calm.

"You're welcome mommy," The doctor said while placing her hand on Presscott's stomach and then continued with, "I want to see you two at 9:30 on Thursday."

"We'll be there." Presscott said as she walked over to her sister to greet her with a big hug.

"Oh baby girl you are such the perfect sight for extremely sore eyes." She said to Halcyon.

Halcyon held Presscott's hands and pushed her away looking at her stomach and said, "Please tell me what I am assuming is true?"

"Six weeks." She said smiling big.

"Oh Scottie...can I kiss him/her?" Halcyon asked.

"You are so silly..." the other two sisters walked in while Halcyon was kissing Presscott's stomach.

"Ooo Scottie, me and Han tried to tell you." Then McKenzie moved Halcyon out of the way while saying, "Move they need some shuga from the favorite auntie."

Hannah hugged Presscott from the back and whispered in her ear, "Congratulations love."

Presscott whispered thank you back while kissing Hannah on her cheek.

They laughed and talked about nothing and came up with a baby dance.

Sean allowed the sisters to visit with one another for about an hour before he broke up the re-union. All four of the siblings were driven to a room with charts and flat screen monitors on the walls. There was a huge beautiful dark cherry wood table in the center of the room. There were three people in the room with name tags that read: Nikko, Juan and Nina. Halcyon immediately turned to Sean and squinted her eyes at him. He ignored her on purpose.

Sean started with, "I had this facility built for you siblings because your father is crazy and I am madly in love with his youngest daughter. This is your situation room. You all will spend a lot of time in here because Stanley has a plethora of things that has to be undone. So without further delay, Nikko I give you the floor." Sean left the conference room.

"Hey I'm Nikko, your oldest brother." He bowed to Presscott then continued, "Presscott you are the oldest sibling. There are five months between us. McKenzie you're next. Juan has Hannah by two days. Halcyon you have Nina by a year and a half. McKenzie you are not Elizabeth's daughter. Your biological mother's name is Juanita."

The silence in the situation room was very thick.

"The four of you were never supposed to know about the three of us other children, but Juan and I wanted to meet our other siblings."

"And what about you Nina?" McKenzie cut Nikko off and asked Nina inquisitively.

"If I never met you all it would have been too soon for me." Nina said staring McKenzie in the eye."

"Prey tale why?" McKenzie asked.

"I don't do well with rich pompous assholes." She said still staring down McKenzie.

"Well Miss Nina my pompous ass will give you a week before I beat yo ass. I'm your big sista, lil girl you don't have the right to disrespect anybody in this room."

"Kennie no..." Hannah was cut off by Presscott.

"Not this time Han." Presscott said.

Then Nina directed her death stare towards Presscott and said, "Bitch I don't like none of you."

She was so busy staring at Presscott that she did not see Halcyon get up and walk over to her. Halcyon grabbed her by the back of her head and said to her face to face, "Understand something, Presscott is NEVER the bitch. Presscott is who you quietly aspire to be like. Presscott is the only one that can keep me off your ass. You don't open your mouth again until you understand respect." Halcyon let her go very roughly.

Then Nina swung on Halcyon and Halcyon beat the mess out of Nina. When Halcyon was done she helped Nina off of the floor and said, "Welcome to the family."

They all just kind of laughed to themselves and then McKenzie asked, "Where did THAT come from Cy Tyson?"

"Don't fu with Scottie in front of me." Halcyon said breathing easy.

Then all of the attention went to Nina.

Presscott then moved her chair right next to Nina's and asked, "Where is all of this coming from?"

She did not answer, she just cried. Presscott pulled Nina into her lap and rocked her back and forth while she cried.

Once Nina calmed down, Presscott said, "Nikko, go ahead with the information you were telling us."

Nikko nodded his head and said, "McKenzie, are you aware of who Juanita Reyes is?"

"Yeah, the first Latin American to dance with the Alvin Ailey dance troop..."

Nikko interrupted her by saying, "She is also your biological mother."

"Boy, don't play with my emotions. I'm already tripp'n about the three amigos being my siblings." McKenzie responded.

Then the door opened and the great Juanita Reyes walked in assisted by a cane. McKenzie stood in respect and reverence and just stared at her. Hannah and Halcyon helped assist her to a seat next to McKenzie.

"Oh my beautiful baby girl." Juanita kept touching her face. "I have longed for this day. I thought it would never come."

"This is such an honor. I have studied your dance for as long as I can remember." McKenzie said in awe of her mother? "Mudear insisted that I knew everything about you."

"Yes, she promised me that you would know of me. She also promised me that she would take care of you best." Juanita said.

"And she did take care of me the best." McKenzie reassured her mother.

McKenzie spent a life time wishing that Mudear was not her mother and hating her. How was she going to make up for this?

The door opened again and in walked Mudear. McKenzie got to Mudear first and said, "How do I apologize to you? I didn't believe the birth certificate you gave me."

Mudear smiled and said, "Don't apologize for the past, just move forward living better."

McKenzie hugged Mudear tight and asked, "Why did you treat me so well and Scottie so badly?"

Mudear was going to have to answer this question truthfully even though she did not want to, "Well I was beaten and my life was threatened if I didn't treat you best." The room was silent and everyone was a little teary eyed. "I eventually confessed everything to Nonny who assisted me in getting the last face lift. She is also the one helping me to create a relationship with Butterfly."

"Who beat you and threatened your life?" Juan was getting angry.

"Your father, Stanley."

Everyone knew the answer to that question but did not want to believe it. Now the unfortunate truth had to be dealt with.

Mudear broke the mood with the clap of her hands and declaring, "We have a lot of work to do, where do we start?"

Nikko cleared his throat and said, "Presscott I did not kill Jonathan, he is here in this facility."

Nina moved back to her own chair. Presscott just stared at Nikko and then he continued, "Mr. Ellington gave the order to kill you, to make Jonathan really kill Anthony. The reason that came down is because Mr. Ellington thought you knew about me, Juan and Nina."

"Presscott did not know about you all but I knew in great detail." Hannah admitted.

"Han we keep underestimating you. How did you know?" McKenzie inquired.

"The night I was in the archives I found a lot of 'stuff' that I just did not mention to anyone." She took a breath and then said, "I honestly thought Anthony was dead and that night I learned that Stanley was behind it."

"Why didn't my father want us?" Nina asked.

"Because according to the bylaws that were set for our family over a hundred and thirty-seven years ago, negates the wealth of the Ellington in charge if they are proven to be an adulterer. Everything that the accused accumulated goes to the next Ellington in the line of succession. That person is Presscott. If children are a result of the affair(s), they are not to be shunned but accepted into the fold with nothing but love. I bet that is why Stanley wanted Presscott dead." Hannah speculated as she was connecting facts together in her head.

"Hannah what else have you put together." Halcyon asked.

"Well," she debated within herself how to say this to her mother, "Mudear the rape was a set up."

"What do you mean 'set up'?" Mudear was getting upset.

"Remmington and I started doing some digging around when I found all of those files in the archives. I have proof that Stanley paid Dexter Edward Jenkins, Sr. to rape you. You two did not know that you were already four and half weeks pregnant before the rape. Apparently he was upset about a relationship you had with Jenkins. When Mudear was pregnant with Presscott he would not be intimate with her, so he got with Miss Reyes and had four children. If his infidelity ever came out he was going to put Presscott's conception into play so his first born son could take leadership."

"He is truly not wrapped too tight." McKenzie said.

"What I really can't figure out is why the Reyes' are on our side?" Hannah looked at the three of them questioning them with her eyes.

Juan explained, "Ellington never treated us as his children, in fact he has never seen Nina. Presscott you and Elizabeth are the ones that provided for us all these years after my mother could no longer support us children anymore."

"How do you mean Juan?" Presscott asked.

"Your butler, Marty, is my uncle, my mother's brother. When he told you that he sent his check back home, you started paying him more money. That money came to us. When Elizabeth found out that my mother had been diagnosed with Multiple Sclerosis she made sure that all of my mother's medical needs were taken care of without question." Juan told.

"So without question," Nikko began, "we are willing to pay our debt through loyalty, if you will allow us."

"There is no debt for you all to repay." Halcyon began, "I'm excited to have big brothers and a hot headed little sister."

"Miss Juanita please let us know whatever you need or think you want and we will get it for you. You are no longer alone, we are family." Presscott declared.

Juanita mouthed a thank you to Presscott and Hannah

picked right back up with, "Just so you all know, Remmy and I are working on bringing Stanley down legally, which means Scottie you are the next in line to run things. Are you willing to take that on?"

"Can I give you an answer in two weeks?" Presscott asked.

"Yes you can, and in the meantime I will have all of the legalities drawn up for you. Does anyone have any objections to Presscott leading the Ellingtons?" Hannah asked and everyone turned and looked at Nina.

Nina cleared her throat and said sheepishly, "I don't have any objections."

Hannah instructed Nina to say 'agreed' when all were asked about Presscott. Then Hannah addressed everyone in the room, "Do all agree with Presscott Elizabeth Ellington Chandler leading the Ellingtons if she chooses to accept the responsibility?"

They all agreed simultaneously.

"Okay. Can this meeting be adjourned? I think I'm ready to see my husband." Presscott inquired.

Hannah said, "All that agree raise your right hand."

Everyone raised their hand.

Hannah declared the meeting adjourned.

Presscott studied the map of the facility. She wanted to just walk through and see everything with one goal in mind, finding Jonathan. As she walked through the facility she noticed people stopping to stand at attention and salute her, so she responded the way she saw on a movie with a president, "At ease." That was weird. The space was enormous, it was their own military base, and the Ellington daughters were priority.

As Presscott journeyed on she realized that a set of footsteps synchronized with her own. She looked to her left and smiled at her new younger brother, Nikko, her personal kidnapper.

"Dr. Chandler may I have a moment of your time?" Nikko asked very respectfully.

"Nikko, my name is Presscott. My siblings refer to me as Scottie or Oldest. You are my brother; you may not call me Dr. Chandler in an unofficial setting, understand?" She said very gently.

"Understood," he responded.

"What's on your mind?" Presscott asked.

"You and your family seem so nice and willing to accept my family as your own. Why?" He asked perplexed.

"We are family. Also over time you will learn that just because we grew up with the money, it didn't make our lives better than anyone else. I raised my sisters to accept people for who they are, right where they are. By the way, your other sisters are not so nice." Presscott smiled at him.

"Well I learned today, you don't cross Mrs. Spence." He was remembering what Halcyon did to Nina a little earlier.

"Here's what you don't know. Mrs. Spencer is Cy, and she found out only a few hours ago that I am pregnant. She is the gentile Georgia Peach of the group. She very rarely shows emotions. My mother did something misguided towards me at her wedding and I had to work hard at keeping her contained. There was no merit behind Nina calling me a bitch. I'm okay with it but your other sisters will never be okay with it." Presscott explained.

"Well your brothers are not okay with it either." He re-assured her. Nikko stopped walking and held out his arm to Presscott and said, "I believe this was your intended destination, Mr. Chandler's location."

"Yes it was and thank you Nikko." Presscott gave him a quaint nod.

"Scottie, he really loves you. When you saw me shoot him at your house, the gun I used was an air gun. I aimed the gun next to his head and the sound is defining. He only appeared to be dead." Nikko said very gently.

Presscott walked into the hospital room noticing first all of the machines and then the beeping sounds of the monitors. She so did not want Jonathan to be in any discomfort, she wished it was her in his place. In spite of all the negative facts that surrounded his connection to her father, she really loved him. She did not want to stop him from being a daddy or a husband. She sat down in a chair next to the door and she watched him breath in and out. She placed her chin in the palm of her hand and ached for the last kiss that they shared. She wanted him to wipe all of the pain away the way he wiped her tears away that night. She wanted to touch him, feel him, breathe him but she no longer knew who he was. So she just watched him with nothing running through her mind. She just loved. She sat there for a long time.

She stood up to leave and heard a very faint, "Honey." He was trying to communicate with her. She looked at him and he said, "Honey."

She flagged down a doctor and said, "Mr. Chandler is trying to speak." She was very formal.

A breathing mask was removed from his face. Tubes

were removed from his body and machines were turned off and removed from the room.

"Dr. Chandler he is asking for you." All of the medical personnel in the room then stood at attention and saluted her.

Nonny walked into the room. Embarrassment flushed Presscott's face as she said, "At ease," and she stepped towards Jonathan's bed waving Nonny near.

"Honey," Jonathan said a third time but Presscott spoke over him.

"Shh don't talk. I just want to be near you and your mom is here." She explained.

He then motioned to her to get closer to the bed and she did. He placed his hand on her stomach.

She whispered to him, "This morning the doctor said we're doing fine."

He then whispered to her, "Are we fine?"

"I really want us to be with everything in me." She responded.

Certain realities she just did not want to face right now, like where her husband's loyalties lie. She knew her father and she knew her husband and therefor her knowledge did not leave her in a good place.

twenty-three:

"Hey! Can anyone hear me?!" Michael yelled and banged on the wall. "If this has anything to do with Stanley Ellington, I didn't call McKenzie, she called me damn it!" He took a deep breath and yelled, "I hate all Ellingtons!"

The clicking of the door made Michael quiet down.

Juan walked in and said, "Sir I can't take you out of this room until you promise me that you are not going to hurt yourself."

Michael laughed and said, "Beating yo ass doesn't require me to hurt myself."

"I would advise against that train of thought Sir," Juan said as he opened the door and watched Michael bolt from the room. He tripped on his shoe string and hit the floor face first hard; he writhed and wretched in pain spouting off profanities. Two buffed guys were walking by and helped him up to his feet. Michael snatched his arms from their grip demanding through clenched teeth, "Get off me." The two guys immediately let him go.

"Michael," McKenzie was getting agitated and embarrassed, "let's go to the medic to make sure you are not hurt."

"Why God? Why am I being cursed by this family?"

Michael asked facing upward.

"Michael you are not being cursed, we are trying to help. I know what really happened. My father was wrong." The weight of her words embarrassed her all over again.

That got Michael's attention and then he looked at her stomach. "What happened?" He asked her sincerely. "I don't need to see the medic." He said.

"Let's walk." She said.

He grabbed her hand and they walked. He was dumbfounded when she told him about the body doubles. Then he told her about the train ride back to New York. Then she very shamefully told him about Nova Scotia and the hasty decision to abort the baby. They stopped walking and held each other tight. Then she said, "Presscott is now the head of the Ellingtons, no more Stanley. I also learned that I have two brothers and another little sister and Mudear is not my biological mother."

"Really?" Michael asked

"Yeah, I don't know how to wrap my head around the Mudear shit. The baby thing has got my heart all messed up. Presscott has helped me a lot with coping with the abortion," she said.

"Well Kennie we can work on the baby thing right

now." He said kissing her.

"You just declared that you hate all Ellingtons. Why you wanna get freaky wit one?" She asked.

He started kissing her neck.

"Not here. My quarters are over there," and she pointed in some random direction.

Remmington was brought into the compound along with Detective Brendel and the B.A.U. team out of Quantico. Everything was surreal to Hannah as she moved through the compound. There was much to take in and wrap her head around. Right now her personal goodness was Anthony and Remmington. When Hannah walked into the B.A.U. she saw the victims' pictures posted on the wall. There were boxes of files on the table. There were maps of body dumps and there was recorded testimony being scrutinized. Hannah had never experienced this side of the desk; this was Remmington's style of leg work. Now Hannah was in the trenches too because Halcyon's safety was at stake as well.

"Okay Detective where are we?" Hannah jumped right in.

"Well the more we look into it, Corbin isn't our guy." Detective Brendel said very flatly.

"Yep, I kind of figured that." Hannah said.

"Share your theory Hannah." Detective Brendel inquired.

"Corbin is too easy, too neat and clean. He doesn't feel right, plus I learned some information earlier today that knocks Corbin out for me." She took a breath to think and then she continued, "I have to share that discovery after I inform my family."

"Han my gut is telling me that something bigger is going on. Kiki Combs is involved but Corbin isn't. How many more family files do we need to go through?" Remmington asked.

"About fifteen," Hannah answered.

"Where are they?" Remmington asked.

"Above ground, do you want to go with me?" Hannah asked.

"Can we go to Dolce?" Remmington asked.

"Yes." Hannah answered.

Hannah then turned to Nikko and asked, "Am I clear to go above?"

"Yes, I will escort you to your car and explain your most important new bells and whistles." He said.

"We should be back by five." She said.

Nikko explained everything with the car. While they were on the compound's property, the car drove itself. Nikko programmed the car to go to the Johnson mansion and Dolce in Peachtree City.

As the car drove to the exit of the compound Remmington asked Hannah, "Who is Nikko?"

Hannah looked at her excitedly and said, "He's my new big brother. Can you believe that?"

"No I can't. Where yall been hiding him?" Remmington asked.

"I met him earlier today for the first time, so far I like him." Hannah answered.

"Do you know if he is spoken for?"

"Remmy."

"I'm just asking, what?"

"So Corbin didn't teach you anything?"

"Corbin taught me what an excellent lay he is, now I want another lay. Is your brother single?" Remmington was getting a little testy.

"Look residential ho, I don't know." Hannah responded.

"I wish your sisters could hear how you talk sometimes." Remmington said calming down.

"Why?" Hannah asked.

"Because I think they would be so shocked." Remmington explained and then she said, "IJS."

"Well..." Hannah started, "Here's an OMG for you. Earlier today when I met my older brother, I also met another little sister. That little heffa called Scottie a bitch. Cy Tyson got up without warning and wupped her ass. Do you hear me? Halcyon Joy Spencer wupped her."

"Joe stop lying." Remmington was in shock.

"I don't think I could have made up a lie like that." Hannah said sounding concerned.

"Cy is so sweet and gentle, she's the Georgia Peach." Remmington stated.

"Until you step out of line with Scottie." Hannah finished the thought. "I have a confession Remmy."

"Joe this better not be corny. What is it?" Remmington asked.

"Not corny but a little embarrassing. I have never been more proud of Halcyon. I didn't know she had it in her to defend someone that she loved like that." Hannah said.

"Really? All of yall are touched when it comes to each other." Remmington chuckled and then continued with, "Remember in high school when Jeremy Slater tried to be our boyfriend at the same time. McKenzie cornered me in the hall and said 'If you weren't Hannah's best friend, I would get expelled today behind yo ass.' And then here come Cy saying all proper like, 'You f'n with the wrong E's.'" Both of them laughed because they both remembered.

"Oh my little baby girl..."

Remmington cut her off with, "She ain't no baby no more she 'f'n' now." They both cringed at the thought and got a good laugh.

twenty-four:

Presscott had a lot of questions about taking charge of the Ellington Empire. She now has three new siblings. Her and McKenzie don't have the same mother. Someone may be trying to kill her baby sister. She now has an underground city that is in her control until she decides otherwise. She doesn't even want to think about the issues with her husband. She needed a nap. She set her alarm on her cell phone to wake her in two hours. Presscott woke up the next morning with Nonny and Mudear watching over her.

She yawned and stretched before she opened her eyes.

"Good morning butterfly." Nonny greeted her.

"Good morning Nonny." She responded with her eyes still closed and then said, "Hey mommy."

"Hey baby, how are you feeling?"

Mudear was interrupted by Nonny asking, "How did you know Mudear was in here?"

"I am extremely sensitive to my mother's smell. She has been sitting in that chair for six minutes trying not to wake me with her shallow breathing."

They all laughed.

Presscott jumped up suddenly to throw up and her

mommies were right there to help. They cleaned her up and changed her into some clean fresh clothes. Presscott was so grateful that she never took a moment to be embarrassed. Both of the ladies crawled in bed with Presscott to console her. Presscott explained to them what was going on with Jonathan. Nonny was hurt and apologetic to Presscott. When Presscott dozed back off into sleep, Nonny left the room straight on a war path to Jonathan.

When Hannah and Remmington made it back to the compound they went straight to work. Hannah's personal goal was to figure out how Kiki Combs fit in the Ellington web.

"Man whoever killed KiKi is good." Remmington said talking to herself out loud.

"What makes you say that?" Hannah asked.

"I have not found any new evidence in two years; this killer cannot be this clever. It's almost like KiKi could have been collateral damage." Remmington was frustrated.

"Okay." Detective Brendel said, "Then tell me how to chase the rabbit you see."

"I've been looking at all the pictures that her parents gave to us, Kiki's hair is always thick and long."

Detective Brendel opened the file of Kiki's pictures on one of the flat screen monitors and gave Remmington the remote control.

Hannah's full attention was on watching Remmington work.

"Well look at her from when she was five years old until the day her body was in our custody, thick, long and lustrous. Her mother didn't believe it was her daughter because of the hair." Remmington clicked the photos until she got to the image that was determined to be the last image of Kiki alive. "Detective Brendel, why is Kiki considered to be this particular unsub's vic? Is the treatment of the hair apart of his MO?" Remmington was tapping into Dr. Spencer Reid from Criminal Minds.

"Well number one they all resemble Halcyon but let's check the evidence." Detective Brendel said.

As Detective Brendel looked through the evidence he asked Hannah, "Is she always like this?"

Hannah laughed and said, "Yep. This is why the feds keep trying to steal her from me."

"Is that right Director Copeland?" Detective Brendel asked the acting director of the B.A.U.

"That's right detective but she always turns us down..."

"There is no evidence there detective right?"

Remmington interrupted the conversation.

"No there doesn't seem to be. Remmington what are we missing?" Detective Brendel became very serious.

"Wow, I can't believe I didn't catch this earlier. These are mocked photo crime scenes. All of these photos of victims are all Kiki Combs. I have a program here that puts doctored photos back to their original state. Ladies and gentlemen watch the screen and be amazed. Now I'm channeling Penelope Garcia from Criminal Minds."

Every person in the room stopped and watched the screen and it turned out that ten victims were all the same vic, Kiki Combs.

Detective Brendel plopped in a chair and asked, "Hannah can I give you legal guardianship of my family when this is over?"

"What are you talking about?" she asked.

"When I find this sick bastard I am going to kill him with my bare hands." He was very angry.

"Look before the witch hunt starts," Remmington said very loudly, "I need some legal clearances because whoever this is, is high up on the totem pole."

"Oh God, I hope my father is not behind this too." Hannah said to herself out loud.

Well Han you have to apply the rule and push forward." Remmington said. Then they said it together,

"Prepare for the worst and hope for the best."

Nonny walked into Jonathan's room fuming mad. She wanted to snatch him out of the bed and make him explain to her why Butterfly lied to her. She knew in her heart of hearts that Presscott was telling the truth about her son. Nonny and the Third never condoned this type of foolishness from any of their offspring. What in the world made him sell his soul?

"Hey ma," Jonathan said just above a whisper.

"Hey yourself, how are you feeling today?" Nonny was trying hard to keep her anger in check.

"I guess I'm okay. The doctor said today they were going to make me walk after lunch." Jonathan felt his mother restraint and he opted to tip toe around it.

"Oh well good, maybe your father will get to see you walk," she did not care about his progress report. "Jonathan, can you tell me what actually happened to you?"

"I was shot," he answered.

"I know you were shot. Why did you get shot? Where were you when you got shot?" Nonny began to ask.

"I can't tell you that," he answered.

"Well why not?" She asked.

"I have to talk to Scottie first," he answered.

"No you don't. You have been lying in that bed for a day and half and you still don't have your lie together? Ever since I listened to Butterfly this morning I have been repenting for the way your father and I raised you. How does one begin to think it is okay to sign his life away in a contract with impossible terms for money? Seriously Jonathan, how stupid are you?"

"I need to talk to Scottie."

"Why do you need to talk to me first Jonathan?" Presscott asked as she walked into the room with Mudear.

How was Jonathan going to get out of this one? His mother, his mother-in-law and his wife stood looking at him waiting for an answer.

"Can I please talk to Scottie alone?" Jonathan asked.

"No you may not." Presscott's answer was in unison with a male voice. Presscott turned to see who the male voice belonged to and she looked right into her father-in-law's face. The Third hugged Presscott, kissed Nonny on the lips and kissed Mudear's hand.

"I need to speak to him privately, would you like to say goodbye to him?" The Third asked the ladies.

Presscott looked at Jonathan and noticed tears falling from his eyes. Then Presscott said, "Sir we will be in the common area when you are done." Presscott then alerted all of the staff that The Third was not to be disturbed during his visit with Mr. Chandler and whatever assistance The Third needed they were to oblige.

The ladies got into a golf cart and drove off.

"Butterfly you just signed your husband's death warrant." Nonny sounded worried.

"No I did not. Your son signed it himself. I'm not worried about The Third, I'm stressed about Jonathan's jail time." Presscott said flatly.

"Jail time for what?" Nonny asked with grave concern.

"Jonathan was supposed to kill Anthony but instead held him hostage and tortured him for two years."

"What?" Nonny and Mudear asked at the same time.

"Take me back to that boy right now Butterfly!" Nonny yelled her request to Presscott.

Presscott turned around with no protest. Nonny jumped off before the golf cart stopped. She walked into Jonathan's room and asked interrupting the very upset The Third,

"Jonathan did you hold Anthony hostage and torture him for two years?"

"Mom I did not kill him," he interjected.

"You identified the body with his wife at the morgue. His wife paid for a lavished funeral. His wife almost starved herself death. Your wife had to readjust her life for her grieving sister. His parents never got over his death. Here is something for you to know, you no longer exist to me." Nonny said that with a broken heart fighting back tears. She walked out of Jonathan's room crushed. She walked through the compound aimlessly.

"Jonathan, I don't know how to respond to that. No wonder your wife is avoiding you. I will get in touch with you when I am ready to talk to you again. You are stripped from everything Chandler until your mother decides to re-instate you." The Third walked out of Jonathan's room heart broken.

The Ellington women, Remmington and Juanita were enjoying each other's company in the common area when Mr. and Mrs. Chandler noticed Hannah. They were all laughing when Hannah heard her name being called. Hannah turned to answer the call but no one in her immediate vicinity was trying to get her attention. She heard the call again and it was getting closer. Anthony walked over to Hannah, kissed her and asked, "Why are you ignoring Nonny?"

"Nonny? Where is she? Is she the one calling me?" Hannah inquired.

Anthony turned Hannah's head in Nonny's direction and said, "Wave her over."

Hannah got up and began to walk over to Nonny and The Third. Hannah greeted them both with hugs and kisses and said, "Scottie is over at the table and Anthony just joined us from his physical therapy session." Hannah knew something was up but she did not want to deal with it without Presscott present, so she led the Chandlers to the table.

"Hey you guys." Presscott stood up to greet them. They just stared at Anthony.

Nonny walked up to Anthony and said, "You used to have beautiful long locks. Your facial features are the same and your eyes are a little murky. How do I know it's really you?" Nonny was in a state of unbelief.

Anthony stood up with Hannah's help. He beckoned Nonny to come closer to him. When she got about an arm's length away he said, "Nonny the mommy you are so beautiful."

She let out a scream of relief and hugged him as tight as she could. The third just stood and watched with one hand over his mouth. There was a gamut of emotions running though his body at one time but the one that was most prominent at this time was embarrassment. He was so hurt that his son was responsible for so much grief.

Anthony reached out to The Third and said, "Mr.

Three can I hug you too?"

No one called The Third 'Mr. Three' except Anthony. Someone else tried to call him that and they got cussed out. The Third hugged him and apologized through tears for what his son did to him.

The Third pulled himself together and asked Anthony and Hannah, "How do we make this right?

Hannah walked over to Anthony and they held each other side by side and Anthony said, "Nonny you are only allowed to keep telling me how beautiful my eyes are. You Sir, I have an idea for a new line of yachts and cruise ships. I need your assistance, if it works then our offspring for the next four generations can be born retired."

"Oh I like the sound of that." The Third declared.

Everyone was introduced to the Chandlers. Everyone was happy and excited but Presscott. She never felt so lonely and afraid; she did not know if her immediate family had a heart beat let alone a life.

twenty-five:

Presscott was exhausted by the time she went to bed. She had finally drifted into a deep sleep and was awakened at 3:41 with the urgency to throw up. She rolled out of bed and desperately tried to make it to the toilet but the bathroom floor had to be sufficient. With no thought in mind, she grabbed a mop, cleanser and towels. She cleaned the entire bathroom. She jumped in the shower and cleaned herself up real good. She brushed her teeth and gargled for the third time. She put on her favorite Jonathan button down shirt to sleep in. She walked back into the bedroom, turned on the light and saw no Jonathan.

She could no longer be strong.

As she slid down the wall to the floor a wailing from deep within her soul was slowly released. She felt just how lonely she was even though she was pregnant. She took a deep breath and grabbed the wall in search of Jonathan's arms to console her, no Jonathan.

Her deep sorrow turned into extreme anger towards God. She began to whisper to God through her tears and clenched teeth, "What did I do to you? Why is this happening to me?"

Her mind was racing through life events while she

caught her breath. Then she said, "I'm the one who was blatantly rejected by her mother. I'm the one who was severely beaten for no reason. I'm the one who always apologizes first and I am normally not involved. God what did I do to you? Haven't I been martyred enough? Now I am pregnant, scared of my husband but I want to fall asleep in his arms. WHAT! DID! I! DO! TO! YOU!?!"

Halcyon woke up at about 4:30 am; she had an uneasy concern about Presscott. She threw on some sweat pants that didn't match her pajama top, no shoes and jogged to Presscott's quarters. She heard her sister yelling, "What did I do to you?" Halcyon became alarmed so she ran into her sister's kitchen and grabbed a frying pan before she made her way to her sister's room. Halcyon peeked into the bedroom looking for the perpetrators. All Halcyon found was Presscott on the floor crying, holding the wall and repeating the question 'what did I do to you?' Halcyon's heart broke. She knew it was bound to happen, she just never thought that she would have the honor to console her big sister.

Halcyon grabbed Presscott's hand and touched Presscott's forehead with her own and said in a whisper, "Hey Scottie it's Cy, what's going on?"

She took a breath between each word and said, "I want my husband."

"Okay, let's go to his room." Halcyon said thinking the problem was solved, easy.

"I will not go." Presscott said as she tried to catch her breath.

"Why not?" Halcyon asked perplexed.

"I don't want to hurt Anthony and Han." She wiped her eyes and face with the sleeves of her shirt and blew her nose with the front shirt tale. Halcyon was disgusted so she went to the bathroom and wet a face cloth with some warm water and soap. She walked back into the room and found a fresh shirt for her sister to put on. Halcyon sat back on the floor in front of her sister and cleaned her face then she asked, "Okay, tell me why we can't go see Jonathan." Halcyon unbuttoned her sister's dirty shirt to find that Presscott didn't have on any panties.

Presscott was explaining why they couldn't go see Jonathan but Halcyon didn't hear it because she was saying her own little prayer, "Okay no more surprises Jesus."

Halcyon got Presscott all changed successfully and they sat in the floor talking. Presscott was very honest with her sister about everything. Finally, someone was there just to listen to her with no preconceived ideas. Presscott fell asleep with Halcyon rocking her.

As soon as Halcyon closed her eyes, Presscott lurched awake and made a mad dash to the bathroom. Halcyon grabbed an overstuffed pillow off of the bed and followed behind Presscott. Halcyon dropped the pillow at the bathroom door and went to the kitchen. She opened the refrigerator and found Cherry Coke and Ginger Ale that was it. She walked back armed with the Ginger Ale. She grabbed a face towel and soaked it with cold water this time. She pressed the cold compress to her sister's face and the back of her neck. She put some tooth paste on Presscott's tooth brush and handed it to her. Presscott brushed her own teeth. Halcyon poured some mouth wash in its bottle cap and handed it to her sister and said, "Gargle, spit, rinse."

After Presscott did that she wiped her mouth and said, "I love you Cy," and she started crying again.

"I love you too," as she wiped her sister's tears away.

"I don't know why I'm crying." She said exhausted.

"Your personal plate just got bigger. You don't know what the future holds for your husband. You're pregnant and hormonal. I would cry too." Halcyon responded.

Halcyon got the pillow and raised the toilet seat.

"What are you doing?"

"You need the toilet and an ear, we may as well get comfortable."

"But you despise the smell of any bathroom."

"And I happen to love you more. Don't worry about it"

Presscott sat in between Halcyon's legs on the floor in front of the toilet. They propped themselves against the tub and the shower door. Halcyon gagged a couple of times but Presscott didn't notice. Halcyon woke up to Mudear gently rubbing her face and softly calling her name. Halcyon woke up putting her finger to her lips then she whispered, "Is Sean here?"

Mudear nodded yes.

She whispered again, "Ask him to come in here please."

Mudear nodded and walked away.

"I'm not asleep." Presscott said.

"Good, I'm going to have Sean put you in the bed." Halcyon stated.

"Are you coming with me?" Presscott asked.

"Yes, after I tinkle." The smell in the bathroom was starting to override Halcyon's gag reflexes.

Sean walked into the bathroom and picked up Presscott and put her in the bed. Halcyon dry heaved a couple of times, used the bathroom, washed her hands, walked out of the bathroom and stepped right into Sean's arms. He pushed her back into the bathroom with a passionate kiss. Halcyon fought hard not to get caught up. She pushed him away and said, "Absolutely not." She stepped into another kiss with him again and quickly pushed him away again and said, "When I get to our quarters, no foreplay I'll be naked." She squeezed his crouch and walked out of the bathroom.

The two sisters slept for the next two hours under the watchful eye of their mother.

twenty-six:

Hannah loved being near her husband. She did not like being away from him if she did not have to be. She propped herself on her hands in the mornings and just stared into his eyes.

"Anthony you know what?" she asked him.

"What love?" he asked her.

"Your eyes are clearing up," she said.

"Really?" he asked.

"Really," she answered.

"Will you answer me something honestly?" he asked.

"Always, no matter what," she answered.

"Do you think I should grow the locks back?" he asked.

"Yes," she whispered.

"Why?" he whispered back.

She laid her head on his chest and took a deep breath. Then she answered, "You would torture me with the best sensations with those locks and I want them back."

He smiled and began to lightly touch her face with the tips of his fingers. She closed her eyes and tried to memorize how every touch felt. He placed the palm of his hand on her nose and she began to create figure eights in his palm with the tip of tongue.

"Hannah if you keep that up, you might get pregnant," he said playfully.

"I dare you to try it," as she straddled him and started kissing him.

He was having issues with getting an erection so he vowed to always communicate with her when the mood was becoming sensual and physical.

"Babe..."

Hannah cut him off by saying, "Let's just live in this moment.

They kissed, they fondled, they caressed, they licked, he penetrated.

"Babe..." She was excited and shocked at the same time.

Anthony cut her off by saying, "Sshh, let's just live in the moment."

And they lived in this moment for a while.

She never noticed herself smiling ever during sex, but during this time she never stopped smiling. Anthony was definitely back.

Presscott woke up from her rough night ready to talk to her husband. She was ready to force issues with him whether he was ready or not. She deserved answers and she was not leaving his room until she was done. So she grabbed Halcyon's hand and off they went.

When they walked into the room, Jonathan was sitting up on the bed. Presscott was so happy to see him doing better.

"Can I say hello to our baby?" he asked

Presscott walked over to his bedside and he touched her stomach. He then pulled her in between his legs and started kissing her stomach. She pulled away from him clearing her throat.

"Please don't pull away I miss you so bad," he said with urgency.

"Uh, you have no idea how much I understand that statement," she responded.

"Are you ready to talk to me yet?" she asked him.

"No, but I no longer have that luxury, so let's hash it out," he said.

"Cy I need you to stay," she said as she pulled a chair next to Jonathan's bed.

"Okay," Halcyon answered as she pulled out a recording device to record the conversation. She also opened the notepad file in her phone to take notes.

"Did you sign the son-in-law contract?" she began the conversation with a question.

Jonathan danced around the answer and Presscott

had no idea that it was this hard for Jonathan to tell the truth. After about an hour of getting nowhere with him she decided to leave and she was extremely frustrated. Right before she walked out of the room she turned to Jonathan and said, "I don't know what changed but I would love to have my husband back. I don't want to raise our child alone."

"When I am cleared to leave here, where do I go?" Jonathan asked her.

Presscott and Halcyon looked at each other with unbelief. Halcyon grabbed Presscott's hand and said, "Come on love, let's go."

When Presscott got back to her quarters Mudear and Nonny were there waiting for the sisters to get back. Because the two mothers were there with Presscott, Halcyon left and promised to be back by 7:30 that evening.

Presscott did not say much, she paced a lot and put Speak To Me by Mary Mary on repeat on her IPod. She wanted definite clarification on some things that she really needed to address her family on. She decided to go for a jog through the compound. She jogged for about forty-five minutes before she realized where she was, in front of Jonathan's room. She took a deep breath and walked in the room. Jonathan was asleep.

"Jonathan," Presscott called his name sweetly and softly three times before he stirred awake.

"Hey Ellington," he said as he cleared his throat. He has not called her that since their wedding day. "What are you doing here?" Jonathan continued with his question to her.

"I wanted to see if you were up to talking, it's just you and I," she said to him.

"Okay we can do that," he said to her.

Presscott jumped right in with, "Are we too far gone for us to work out?"

"I believe we are," he answered.

"Will you explain to me why you think we cannot work it out?" She slipped in Psychology mode to try and protect herself.

"What I am about to explain to you is really going to hurt you. I understood that hurting you was a possibility but I never imagined this much. I do apologize for that."

Presscott did not interrupt; she just sat in the chair next to his bed and listened.

He continued with, "I was groomed by your father and Dexter Edward Jenkins, Sr. to be your mate once your father found out for sure that you were his child. I was to marry you and convince you to emancipate yourself from the family. He could have never predicted that you and your sisters were going to become as inseparable as you guys are. Your brother Nikko was the answer to your emancipation. I was ordered to fall in love with you and follow every order that I received from your father. Anthony and I became friends so I could not follow through with his kill orders. I got orders to kill you but you told me you were pregnant and I am truly in love with you. Every time I see you, I fall deeper in love with you. You make logic make sense and I want you all the time. I have orders right now to kill you on site but I just cannot."

Presscott understood every word he said and she stayed quiet as she continued to absorb the words that he said.

"The only thing I ask you to remember is the name Kiki Combs."

She did not indicate that she already knew about Kiki Combs. Presscott stood up and kissed Jonathan on the forehead goodbye.

Jonathan was shocked at her calm response.

Presscott got back to her quarters in time to see Nikko walk in, that was the person she wanted to see. Presscott walked in and Nikko, Nonny and Mudear were visiting with one another in her living room.

"Hey everyone," Presscott was trying to be as

pleasant as she could. She was greeted with hugs and kisses from everyone. "Well," Presscott began, "I have decided that Jonathan and I are no longer a couple. He has decided that his loyalties have been and will continue to be served somewhere else."

Nonny immediately started fussing defending Presscott's honor. Nikko did not say a word. Mudear just watched Presscott very closely.

"Nikko, will you get word to all of the siblings to meet here with me tonight at 8:45." Then she called up the control room and asked them to cue up the audio and video from her last visit with Jonathan. She wanted it to play in her quarters only for her siblings when they all met.

twenty-seven:

Mr. Ellington paced back and forth in his private conference room.

"Nikko do you know anything about Presscott's or Jonathan's whereabouts?"

"No sir." Nikko answered with ease.

"Presscott is not that clever to hide in plain sight and Jonathan has been trained to do what he is told." Mr. Ellington was talking out loud randomly. Then he asked, "Didn't you report to me that Jonathan was shot?"

"Yes sir I did." Nikko answered.

"What happened to the body?" Mr. Ellington asked.

"Sir I was not a part of clean up because I joined the search for Presscott." Nikko said.

"What exactly did you find in the house?" Mr. Ellington asked.

"A hidden garage that is not on the blueprints of the house Sir." Nikko answered.

"Well what did you find in the garage Nikko?" Mr. Ellington asked through clenched teeth and frustration.

"Sir there was nothing in the garage." Nikko answered very easy.

"Jonathan's body hasn't turned up anywhere, so I cannot safely conclude that he's dead. Presscott doesn't have the street smarts to evade me. Hannah is never a problem. McKenzie hates Michael right now because of an abortion. Everybody hates Mudear, so I am not worried about her. Where is Juan and Nina?" Mr. Ellington asked Nikko while he tried to get mental tabs on all of his children.

"Juan and Nina got picked up to be personal body guards for a high profile family Sir." Nikko answered.

"Which high profile family?" Mr. Ellington asked.

"They cannot disclose that information as of yet Sir." Nikko answered.

"Nikko do you think you can get me an answer about Presscott and Jonathan by the end of the week?" Mr. Ellington was pissed off.

"I am working on it Sir." Nikko answered.

"You're dismissed." Mr. Ellington said calculating his next move.

When Nikko left the conference room, Mr. Ellington activated the intercom and said, "Put a tale on Nikko."

Nikko heard the command because he hid two bugs in the conference room earlier that day. Nikko called Juan and said, "Ellington is putting a tale on me...right, right, left, left, right."

"Ten four, we will be there in five." Juan said.

"Tell Nina this one is all courtesy of dear old dad."

They laughed and then disconnected.

The siblings listened to the last time Presscott and Jonathan talked and they decided that The Third and Nonny should decide what happened to Jonathan. Nikko did warn them that if they sent Jonathan back to Mr. Ellington he would be killed. Nikko then explained how he, Juan and Nina inserted themselves as moles in Mr. Ellington's camp. The control room at the compound always had eyes and ears on them whenever they were within Ellington's camp.

Presscott wanted Hannah to find out what was happening with the Wells side of the family. Presscott and Mudear would find the bylaws for the Wells. Presscott wanted to get to know her mother's side of the family. All of the siblings gave McKenzie their blessings on a potential marriage between her and Michael.

The siblings stayed in Presscott's quarters talking. They made collective decisions. They agreed and disagreed. Hannah found out Nikko was single for Remmington. They all threw up with Presscott. All seven of them slept in Presscott's bed. The mothers woke them around 10:30 that morning.

twenty-eight:

Remmington awoke and quietly disappeared into the situation room still wearing her PJ's. She kept hearing Jonathan in her head telling Presscott to 'remember the name Kiki Combs.' She used her FBI clearance to find out the IP address on the doctored Kiki Combs crime photos. When she finally got the name she felt sick to her stomach. She printed out the blueprints of the building of where the IP address originated from along with the address of the building. This was bad, this was real bad. Her whole body ached as she made her way back to Presscott's quarters.

Nonny noticed Remmington first and she asked, "Remmy baby what's wrong?"

Everyone got quiet and all of the attention went to Remmington. Remmington looked at Presscott and handed her the address and the blueprints. Presscott looked at the blueprints and said, "This is Chandler mansion."

Remmington was very uneasy as she brought out the blueprint with the circled location, pointing to it she asked, "Can you tell me where this is?"

Presscott looked at the blueprint and said, "Let's see. This is the west wing, second floor, far east this is

Jonathan's office suite."

"No, no, no damn it! No!" Hannah yelled; she was very angry.

"What's wrong Remmy?" Presscott asked.

"I think you all should sit down and Han call Brendel."

Remmington knew this was not going to go over well so she tried to remove all of her emotions out of the explanation. "Two days ago we discovered the pictures of all the victims from the Kiki Combs case are the same person. The pictures of one victim were doctored to look like multiple victims and at multiple crime scenes. We thought we were looking for a serial killer and we are not. We needed to find out where these pictures originated from and Presscott you just confirmed the location."

Nonny asked, "What does this mean?"

"This means it is very likely that Jonathan knows who the killer is and why Kiki Combs was killed." Remmington was very uneasy as she tried to read Presscott's emotions.

"Hannah, why are you so upset?" Nina asked.

"I personally represent the Combs. Jonathan is my brother-in-law and the law says this is a conflict of interest. I now have to be recused or removed from the case. My firm is going to prosecute every person involved with this case to the fullest. I don't want to cause Scottie or Nonny any more pain, but it seems like the more we uncover the facts, the more we discover Jonathan is a serious bad guy. I don't want that for Scottie. Damn it." Hannah was livid.

Everyone understood that, so the room just remained quiet.

Detective Brendel, Sean and Nikko went to talk to Jonathan with Nonny and The Third.

"Jonathan you are under arrest for your involvement with the murder of Kiki Combs. Your wife has given the APD permission to search your personal office suite in your home. Do you have any objections thus far Mr. Chandler?" Detective Brendel was very professional.

"No sir I don't." Jonathan said flatly.

"Mr. Chandler due to your admission of working for Stanley Preston Ellington, it has been decided that you will be held in custody within this compound for your safety. Do you have any questions?"

"Why is my safety a concern?" Jonathan asked.

"I have been given the order by Mr. Ellington to kill you if I find you alive." Nikko said bluntly.

"If you would like to take a chance in lock up above

ground, we will not object." Detective Brendel said.

"I will stay here Sir." Jonathan said.

"You have the right to remain silent. Anything you say can and will be used against you in a court of law. You have the right to speak to an attorney, and to have an attorney present during any questioning. If you cannot afford an attorney, one will be provided for you. Do you understand these rights Mr. Chandler?" Detective Brendel asked.

"Yes sir I do understand my rights. I do not need an attorney provided." Jonathan's words were very sterile, he felt like he could not show any signs of weakness. Then he asked, "May I speak with my parents privately before I am detained?"

Detective Brendel gave an affirmative nod and Nonny walked out with everyone else leaving The Third and The Fourth to speak to one another.

Jonathan said, "I only have one question." The Third looked at him with great frustration and remained silent.

Then Jonathan asked, "Will you please make sure that my child is well taken care of?"

"Why would I have to make sure of that?"

"I want my child to know who I am."

"Well Jonathan seeing as how no one knows who you are, how do we explain who you are to a child?"

"Dad," Jonathan's words were cut off by his father.

"Only my children call me 'dad'. Why don't you get in touch with Mr. Ellington since that is who your loyalties lie with?" The Third took a beat for the thought to sink in then he began to walk out of Jonathan's room and said, "But Mr. Ellington has a bounty on your head."

Jonathan was then removed from his hospital room and detained in the compound's lock up.

Halcyon sat at the monitors inside the Free Running facility and watched Presscott workout. She never knew that her big sister was into free running and she was good. There were several times Halcyon thought that Presscott was going to break a bone but it was part of the routine. She really liked her work on the uneven bars because her dismount would lead her running up a wall, across a rail, through a tunnel and onto a trampoline. Halcyon tired from watching her but she could not stop watching her. Presscott finally stopped to pace, think and drink some water.

Halcyon walked over to her big sister and said, "Wow you looked great out there. I would have never guessed that you would have found time for free running."

Presscott chuckled and said, "I didn't think I had time either until I had a patient that was obsessed with it. My patient challenged me to just watch a movie on Netflix about it and see if I didn't get hooked. I'm hooked and yes sometimes my patient and I free run through Midtown, Buckhead, Decatur and anywhere else we feel challenged to do so."

Halcyon squinted her eye at her sister and said, "I never put danger in your make up. You have always been the protective one, fore seeing all the danger ahead."

"And I believe that is why I enjoy it so much. If I get caught up in what may happen, I could die. If I get caught up in what did happen, I probably will die. My mind has to be completely focused on the present. The past has happened, I can't change it. The future depends on my present; that is where I need to focus." Presscott explained, and then she said, "It was also a great relief from Mudear and her shenanigans."

They both laughed.

"What went down with you and Mudear at my wedding?" Halcyon asked.

Presscott hated that transition of subjects but she didn't skip a beat, she just answered truthfully. "Remember how you needed something new, something blue and something borrowed?"

"Yes." Halcyon was anticipating the stupid answer.

I planned for your new and blue and completely

forgot about the borrowed. You kept talking about the lip gloss I was wearing that day, it matched everything perfectly. So we wiped off your lipstick and I let you borrow my lip gloss."

Halcyon started talking over Presscott, "So she almost ruined my wedding because you let me borrow your lip gloss?"

"Yes." Presscott said cautiously because she did not know how her baby sister would react.

Halcyon shook her head and said, "Wow Scottie you put up with so much unnecessary stuff." She took a breath and then asked, "So now you have no hard feelings towards her even though she made your life as hard as she did?"

Presscott considered her answer and said, "I think it is safe to say that I have mixed feelings towards her. I turned out to be a Psychologist, I deal with issues differently. When someone does something, I want to know why. I think to deal with my own feelings about Mudear; she has become a case study for me. Right now it looks like all is forgiven and we are just tip toeing through the tulips, but I have to deal with and process a lot right now. Mudear is only a fraction of my whole. Does that make sense to you?"

"It does make sense to me but I don't want it to. Our

mother did not take much interest in me unless it was going to hurt you. When I was a kid I used to walk around with a dictionary so I could understand the grown up conversations that were being said in the house. The more I heard and understood, the closer I got to you. You are so safe. I went into Interior Design originally to learn how to create a perfect space for you devoid of Mudear." Halcyon's thoughts were very genuine and raw.

Presscott hugged her sister and said, "Aw baby girl that is so sweet." Presscott took a beat and then asked, "Can you add a plus one in my space?" She tapped her stomach and smiled.

"Anything for you Scottie, okay show me some of this Free Running stuff."

Presscott shook her head and said, "We only have about an hour because I have to figure out how to run an empire."

They both smiled and began the first workout.

twenty-nine:

The time was now 1:45 and all of the siblings were in the Situation Room. Presscott was smartly dressed in some straight legged khaki colored linen pants tapered at her waste, some low black leathered pumps, a wide black leather belt with a silver buckle highly polished, a high collared pure white button down shirt and all of her accessories were high polished silver. Presscott was dressed for battle and failure was not an option; now she needed to figure out how to get it done effectively.

"Damn Scottie, you look and smell wonderful. What are you wearing?" McKenzie chimed in right when Presscott walked in the room.

"Thank you younger. We can talk about the 'girl stuff' later. I have a very specific agenda right now, and I don't want to get side tracked, fair?" Presscott responded to everyone looking at McKenzie.

They all said "fair" wondering what was going to happen next because they had never seen this Presscott.

"Okay, first I would like to say is thank you for showing up. We have a lot of things to tackle in order for us to move forward appropriately with our individual lives. For example, I would like to personally live above ground again." Presscott looked at everyone as she spoke and so far they all silently agreed with the nodding of their heads. Presscott had a folder under her arm that only had six sheets of paper in it. She opened the folder and handed out today's agenda.

"Here we go." Presscott said as she officially began the meeting. "I, Presscott Elizabeth Ellington Chandler, accept the role of being the leader of The Ellington Empire. I vow to keep the bylaws of The Ellington family intact. I vow to make sure that all of the Reyes children that were fathered by Stanley Preston Ellington will be taken care of. I vow to thoroughly scrutinize the Ellington bylaws to make sure they are current to the existing time. I declare that the bylaws may not be changed unless the Ellington/Reyes children all agree alike. This say I."

All of the siblings stood and clapped in acceptance.

"All in favor say 'I'". Hannah asked all in attendance.

Everyone said, 'I'.

"Are there any 'nays'?" Hannah asked.

The room fell silent. Hannah continued with, "Dr. Chandler, you have been unanimously voted in as the new leader of The Ellington Empire. Congratulations Madame."

"Thank you Esquire." Presscott said and nodded a cordial acceptance. Presscott took a seat and looked at the agenda for the day.

"Esquire I need you to get me a copy of the most current bylaws for The Ellingtons and The Wells. Nikko, do you know if the Reyes family has bylaws setup?" Presscott asked her brother.

"I don't know." Nikko said sheepishly.

"That's quite all right. Esquire?" Presscott said without looking at Hannah.

Hannah was writing notes on a legal pad as she answered, "Got it."

Presscott continued, "Nikko, tell me the chain of command with Ellington underground."

Nikko cleared his throat and said, "You are the only person that can override Commander Percy Red, Sean Spencer, myself..."

Presscott interrupted him with this question, "Do you think it is possible for the three of you to have a meeting with me today at 5:30 this evening?"

"Yes. Where would you like the meeting to take place?" Nikko asked.

"The Combat Situation Room. I apologize for cutting you off a moment ago, is there anyone else in command I need to know about?" She asked.

"Commander Red, Mr. Spencer and myself are the top three running Ellington underground. Before this meeting is over I will have a copy of everyone's rank and post delivered to your quarters." Nikko was very professional.

Presscott then turned to McKenzie and asked, "Kennie can you find out how the investigation is going for Lance?"

"Sure. Are you looking for anything in particular?" McKenzie asked.

"I probably won't know the answer to that until you report." Presscott answered.

"Okay." McKenzie responded.

"Nina, what are your strengths?" Presscott asked her.

"I'm a black belt in three different Marshal Arts; I'm a Free Runner and Michael's bodyguard."

They all found humor in the last admission then Presscott said, "I'm a Free Runner as well, meet me in the free running facility at 10:00 tonight. I want to see what you got."

"Okay." Nina was excited because now she was free to beat her pregnant sister.

"Juan, where do your strong points rest?" Presscott asked.

"Well, I am a dancer, I have a black belt in two different Marshal Arts and I also free run. Unique to me is that I am the family nerd and I have the ability strategize whatever is needed."

"Okay, excellent. This is what I am thinking, please feel free to object. Now that I have a more clear understanding of who is at the table, it seems that the 'Ellingtons' are very secure and accurate with 'paper pushing'. The 'Reyes' are more comfortable with the physical. McKenzie when it comes to the Ellington Empire 'stuff' I would like for you to be the liaison between the siblings." Presscott waited for a moment to see how her sister would bite.

McKenzie responded with, "If I am completely honest, Hannah should be your liaison."

"Why?" Presscott asked.

"Han at least lives in the state. You gave me a job already with Lance, let me complete that one first. Please." McKenzie pleaded.

"Esquire, what say you?" Presscott asked Hannah.

"May I defer that responsibility to Halcyon?" Hannah asked.

"Why?" Presscott asked.

"With all of the legal responsibilities that I have already, I would rather not take on anything else not pertaining to law. Besides, Halcyon has the ability to communicate with anyone on any level. She has a very objective head on her shoulders. She is very trustworthy, she is clever. She is beautiful. She does not have an official assignment yet." Hannah explained.

"Halcyon, what say you?" Presscott asked Halcyon?

"I accept." Halcyon responded.

"All in favor say 'I'." Hannah addressed all of the attendees.

They all said 'I'.

"Are there any nay sayers?" Hannah asked.

The room fell silent.

Hannah continued with, "Congratulations Halcyon Joy Ellington Spencer you have unanimously been voted in as the official Family Liaison between the siblings."

There was a cordial nod between Hannah and Halcyon of acceptance.

"Now, Esquire I know that you recused yourself from Jonathan's case, are you recused from any other cases involving family?" Presscott asked Hannah.

"I cannot legally have anything to do with any of the family issues. Remmington will cover everything except Kiki Combs and Corbin Wolfe. Another high ranking partner will take over that portion and I will have nothing to do with that at all. Therefore all of the legal questions should be directed to Remmington." Hannah was formal, sterile and hurt. She felt like she could not help her family legally in any way.

"I would like for Remmington to no longer work on

the case until she is cleared by the judge assigned on the case. She is equivalent to a sibling and I don't want any technicalities to come into play." Presscott waited for an acknowledgement from Hannah.

She nodded in discuss and then Presscott continued, "Just so you all know, Jonathan was detained and is being held here in lock up. It was approved by a Fulton County judge in an attempt to protect him from Ellington. You all heard my last conversation with him therefore you know who he is aligned with, Stanley. Nikko has been tasked by Ellington to make sure I am dead and to kill Jonathan if he is found alive." Presscott was interrupted by McKenzie.

"So Nikko we need to fear you too?" McKenzie asked blatantly.

"McKenzie I am a mole. I try to make sure that I am the only person tasked to eliminate Ellingtons. I was supposed to kill Jonathan and I was the witness that convinced the judge to keep him in hiding. The only reason I have not killed Ellington yet is because I have not figured out you all's feelings about him." Nikko was very direct.

Presscott continued with, "As far as Jonathan and I are concerned, I don't know what to do. I am pregnant with his child. I could snuff out his life with one word. If I take him at his word and nothing else, I was just an assignment, he never loved me. The psychologist in me says that his words are a defense mechanism because the physical love we shared can't be faked. Times that we shared in conversation only can't be faked. Times that we shared with family can't be faked. The laughter we shared can't be faked. The last kiss we shared was not faked, so I feel like I am just floating where Jonathan is concerned. I don't want to decide anything, where ever chips fall, that's where they lay."

"Why are you so sure that he's safe here? Listening to you being that vulnerable about his dumb ass makes me want to snuff him out myself with or without your word." McKenzie was upset.

"Well from the stories I have heard about how Mudear treated you and now your husband saying what he said, Jonathan's "snuffing out" can be taken care of without your knowledge." Nina said while she was thinking things through. "I got beat for calling The Great Presscott out of her name and he gets away with this because he was a good lay? I don't get it, enlighten me please."

"Jonathan is not getting a slap on the wrist. Once everything is out on Jonathan, his life may be taken from him legally and The Great Presscott will have no say in the matter. Nina, have you ever been in love?" Halcyon asked.

"No." Nina responded.

"Let's revisit this conversation when you're in love and the make it or break it thing happens and you are faced with the permanent decision. I invite everyone to come to my house for that ice-cream party. Love changes the game." Halcyon explained.

"Right is right and wrong is wrong. Love shouldn't change that." Nina expressed.

"Maybe in your perfect world, but we don't live in your perfect world. In my perfect world Simone is the sun, moon, stars and everything in between." Juan said as he reminisced.

Everyone was shocked that Juan spoke up.

"Didn't you two break up like some years ago?" Nina asked annoyed.

"Four years, seven months, three weeks, one day to be exact." Juan said.

"She is married with children, let it go already." Nina said.

So Nina let's say you are with someone and things are going great. You are contemplating the next level with him. You have admitted to yourself that you love him and boom the make it or break it situation occurs, what do you do?" Nikko asked Nina.

Presscott wanted to stop this conversation and get back on task but all of the siblings were talking about love, she was not going to stop the flow.

"That's easy, I would walk away." Nina was sure of herself.

Hannah finally chimed in, "Oh young one, you have truly never been in love before. Love turns everything upside down. There is no rhyme or reason with love."

"Nina if you were me, how would you deal with Jonathan?" Presscott asked.

"He would be no more." Nina said.

"Just that simple?" Presscott asked.

"Yes." Nina said.

"Then I would dare to conclude that you will never be in love." Presscott said.

"That is so final and cruel, why would you conclude that?" Nina asked.

Dr. Chandler explained, "Love is about being with someone honestly with no conditions. Love looks over faults and looks for ways to try again. Love wants to kiss and make up. Love says no matter what, I'm here. Sometimes love will say walk away. Love always fights for the heart. You precious one have already decided it's my way or the highway. You have lost the game before it started."

"Let the church say what?" McKenzie yelled the question to everyone.

Everyone yelled back in response, "Amen," in unison.

Then McKenzie said, "Nina let me attempt to explain it to you on a physical level. When you have that first bomb orgasm with your dude, he becomes the opposite of anything considered wrong. All of your deal breakers fade to black."

No one said anything at first because they were all mentally transported back to that first bomb orgasm.

"Wow siblings I think we had our first true bonding moment. I hate to do this, but we have to refocus and keep working through the agenda." Presscott said.

They all agreed and worked for the next two hours trying to hash things out appropriately.

5:30 on the dot Presscott walked into the Situation Room and the three gentlemen saluted her. "At ease gentlemen," she said still feeling very awkward.

"Dr. Chandler this is Commander Percy Red." Nikko made the introduction.

As Presscott reached out her hand as a salutation she said, "It is a pleasure meeting you Commander Red," she took a beat and then continued with, "I am guessing that this should take no more than an hour if we get started now."

All three of the gentlemen concurred and Presscott started with Commander Percy, "Commander Red I have had a moment to skim through your biography and it is nothing short of amazing with all of your accomplishments as a Navy Seal, why did you chose to come to Ellington underground?"

"Well, it was a personal move for me," he began. "Some thirty three years ago I was a bad guy for Dexter Edward Jenkins, Sr. When your mother was kidnapped, I drove the van and I was the one that returned her to your father. I promised myself that I would make things right with your mother. When I returned your mother to your father, he put me in the hospital, when I was released I joined the Navy. Over the years I kept tabs on the Ellingtons and Dexter. I intend on helping you, whether you want my help or not, these are not noble men. I think it is time that you kids truly have someone in your corner. I'm here."

Presscott was impressed with what Commander Red had to say. Then she asked Nikko, "What are your true thoughts on Commander Red?"

"Dr. Chandler."

"No Nikko, I'm your sister now and I need help from my brother," Presscott said when she interrupted Nikko.

"Okay real talk Scottie, Commander Red is the one that devised the plans to keep all the siblings safe along with Mr. Spencer. I am more than honored to be under his command. I will blindly follow him anywhere." Nikko was very sincere.

"Okay, I here you," Presscott began and then she turned her attention to Sean and asked, "What are your thoughts?

"Scottie please give Nikko permission to call me Sean?"

Presscott chuckled and said, "Permission granted."

With Sean's approval from Presscott he said, "I have every confidence in Commander Red to get the job done. He is the one that I consulted for Ellington underground. He is the reason you, Jonathan, Michael and Lance are not deceased. He is also the real reason why Jonathan is detained here."

The room was quiet for about five seconds. Presscott stood up and began to pace. She was very concerned as she carried the weight of her family's safety on her shoulders. She stared at the Commander long and hard as she prayed silently for direction. Then she let out a short quick staccato breath and she asked, "Sir is there a name that you would prefer me to use in this type of setting?"

"Percy." Commander Red answered.

"Okay Percy you are in." Presscott responded.

"Thank you." Commander Red said.

"Don't thank me yet." Presscott said with raised eyebrows.

"Yes ma'am." Commander Red responded.

"Scottie. Do you have a plan to bring down S.P.E.?" Nikko asked.

"Yes, I think so." said Presscott

"What is needed to put it into action?" Nikko asked again.

"You alls approval." Presscott answered.

"When can we see it?" Nikko asked.

"How about no later than 10:00 am tomorrow?" She asked.

"Yes." Nikko answered.

"Can I also have a hard copy of this meeting sent to the sibling quarters within the next twenty minutes.?" Presscott asked.

"Yes." Nikko responded.

"Okay gentlemen, is there anything else?" Presscott made eye contact with each of them. She noticed how Sean and Nikko made eye contact with Commander Red and nodded an approval.

Commander Red cleared his throat and said, "May I have your permission to work with Jonathan?"

"For what reason?" She simply asked.

"I know you are a Psychologist and I also know that Jonathan went through a military grooming in order for him to view you as an assignment. I would like to work with him to get information about S.P.E., Corbin Wolfe and Kiki Combs and see if I can get him to some sort of normal thinking. I need you to monitor the sessions." Commander Red was not sure how Presscott was going to react to his question.

She did not seem to consider the implications of the question before she said, "Thank you for the offer. Let me know when you want to get started and I will plan my schedule accordingly. The first two sessions you will fly solo. They will not be recorded. I don't want to be privy to what may initially come out. My heart needs a break." She took a moment to fight the emotions that wanted to present themselves at the mention of Jonathan's name.

Sean and Nikko noticed Presscott's internal torment.

Presscott cleared her throat and then said, "If there is nothing else, we can adjourn."

The room fell silent.

Presscott looked at her watch and said, "Gentlemen

we are adjourned and that took twenty seven minutes."

9:45 pm Presscott walked into the Free Running facility and she felt at ease. She never expected to enjoy this sport as much as she did. She wondered what her little sister was going to show her, she was excited to finally work with her sister on her playground. Presscott sat on a bench to change her tennis shoes. A piece of paper was dropped on the ground deliberately in her eye site. It was a map of a course that had fifteen flags strategically placed.

"Hey big sis," Nina started, "this is how we begin our workout tonight."

Presscott just looked at the course and then sat up to look at her sister.

"The guys that created the course said the max time for this is fifteen minutes. A minute per flag, do you want to do this?" Nina asked sincerely, giving Presscott an opportunity to back out.

"This should be fun. Do you place a time wager when you compete?" Presscott asked.

"Let's write them down and start in five minutes. Agreed?" Nina asked Presscott.

"Agreed," Presscott repeated and walked over to Halcyon and asked for a piece of paper.

Presscott wrote: *complete course in ten minutes beat Nina by two minutes twenty seven seconds.*

Nina wrote: *complete course in fifteen minutes beat Scottie by ten minutes.*

A starter pistol started the race and the sound of the gun escorted Presscott into a utopia of sorts. The outside world was silenced, every concern that she carried on her shoulders melted away with ease. She came upon the first flag and chose to do a backward flip over it so she could check out Nina's position. Presscott was comfortable with the spacing; she knew her prediction was accurate. Presscott zoned out again because now her race was against the clock.

Nina had a great start but her big sister was turbo extreme. By the time Nina hit her tenth step she saw Presscott do a back flip picking up her first flag. The more she focused on Presscott, the greater the distance between the two increased. Nina did not want an older pregnant woman beating her. Nina ran to her first flag slowing her pace so she could grab her flag.

Presscott was no longer in her line of vision. It seemed like every time Presscott picked up a flag, she got faster. She never slowed her momentum to grab a flag; she twisted, flipped, slid, swung around a pole or plucked the flag while running past its position. Every time Nina picked up a flag, she got slower because she would slow down to get a flag. Free Running 101: never slow your momentum to capture a flag. Presscott crossed the finish line in ten minutes flat. Presscott looked at the monitor and clapped her hands in disappointment. All of the siblings ran over to Presscott to congratulate her on her run. She looked up at Nikko and said, "I lost the wager."

"Looking at the board, can you calculate Nina's time?" Nikko asked.

"14:02." Presscott said disappointedly, she clapped her hands again. She turned her attention to the screen and watched the remainder of Nina's run closely. "She's hurt!" Presscott yelled and immediately began to bark orders. Nina crossed the finish line and her time was 14:02. Once she crossed the finish line she was lifted onto a gurney and whisked away to the medical facilities.

Juan turned to Hannah and asked, "How did Dr. Chandler do that?"

Hannah laughed and said, "That's her little sister."

"But we all just met." Juan continued his inquiry.

"Your oldest sister is a Psychologist, her job is to read people." Hannah tried to explain.

"But how was she so accurate with the times?" Juan wanted to know.

"That I don't know but I will let that be your investigation." Hannah said as she walked away.

The siblings had a make shift celebratory party for Presscott's win. Presscott was with Jonathan mentally. Her heart started yearning for him without her realizing it at first. She wanted to see him, to touch him, he should be here with her. This was the first time that her family saw her run and neither her husband nor her father was there. One gave the order for her death and the other was trying to fulfill the order. Tears had welled up in her eyes and Halcyon and Sean were watching her closely. They both walked over to her and then escorted her to a golf cart. No words were exchanged between the three of them and Sean drove to where Jonathan was being held.

Presscott walked in the facility and made a mental decision to leave the psychologist out of this meeting, she was the wife that needed her husband.

Jonathan was laying on a cot and when he heard the door to the facility open he sat up.

Presscott walked into his cell and the tension grew thick.

He noticed her tear stained eyes. He wanted to ask her what was wrong, but he opted not to.

She grabbed his hand and kissed it. Then she

whispered the question, "Will you please hug me?"

He wanted to reject her? He loved her for real. He wanted their love back. When he looked at her he realized how much everything ached to be with her. He hugged her, he hugged her tight and he melted in her arms. No words were spoken out loud but their hearts spoke volumes to each other.

"Scottie I want us back." Jonathan whispered in her ear.

She refused to respond verbally, she did not want to wake up from this beautiful dream. She felt his hands find their way to her hips and her nipples perked up. He kept whispering words in her ear but she did not want to hear them, so out of a desperate need for quiet she tilted her head up to his mouth and kissed him deep and passionately. She felt his nature rise against her stomach and she thought, *that's your dad*. He cupped her head in his hands and then he stopped suddenly.

No no no this is not ending, then she heard a familiar voice say respectfully but forcefully, "Scottie let your body go limp right now. We got you." She let her body go limp and dropped safely into a pair of arms. She opened her eyes and saw Sean standing behind Jonathan with his hands on Jonathan head ready to snap his neck.

When Presscott was safely out of the cell she heard

Sean say, "I will kill you, do you understand that?"

"That would be the freak accident of the century." Jonathan said very cool.

"If you don't want her don't lead her on." Sean said as he moved his hands from Jonathan's head.

Jonathan took the opportunity to do a beautiful standing backward round house kick aimed at Sean's head. Sean was known for his speed and being extremely calm. So he immediately dropped to one knee and threw a powerful jab to Jonathan's groin area. Jonathan dropped heavy to his knees with both hands grabbing his crouch.

"You just experienced my grace. If you fuck with Scottie again then I kill you." Sean's words were intentional as he walked out of Jonathan's cell.

Presscott did not sleep that night. She knew that she had to step up and start making the hard decisions that no one had the nerve to make; she understood that concept, she didn't want to make them either. She left Commander Red a message to come and see her first thing this morning; this would prove to be the most rational decision that she would make concerning the family.

"Dr. Chandler," Commander Red called her name

as he knocked gently on the front door.

Presscott answered the door and invited the Commander in and offered some tea or Cherry Coke. He declined on both because he was eager to meet every request if he could.

They sat at the dining room table before she began.

"Commander Red, may I be frank Sir?" Presscott asked as she was trying to get her thoughts together, she was very discombobulated.

"Yes ma'am, of course." He answered with no emotion.

"I don't know what to do with Jonathan or my father. I cannot make a rational decision where they are concerned. I really want to make the right choice but my heart gets in the way every time." Presscott took a beat as she considered the question she was about to present to Commander Red. "Sir may I ask you to take over where Jonathan and my father are concerned?"

"Dr. Chandler, are you sure you want to relinquish that power to someone not in the family?" Commander Red asked.

"That's why I am coming to you Sir. The family and I will make emotional decisions and that will benefit no one in the end. I did not sleep last night because I was trying to rationalize Jonathan's last murder attempt on my life.

I need some help, will you help me?" Presscott was pleading for help. She was tired and she wanted to sleep and wanted this part of the Ellington saga to be over.

"Yes ma'am. I will do this for you." He was more than happy to do this job for Presscott.

After the Commander left Presscott's quarters she called Nina via the inter telecommunications system. "Good morning Nina, how is your ankle?" Presscott asked as she talked to the flat screen monitor.

"GM. The ankle is okay. The doctor says it was an unforeseen freak thing and that I have to stay off of it for at least a week. Nothing is broken, sprang or fractured."

"Oh thank God but are you okay though?"

"Bruised ego. I really wanted to beat you."

Presscott chuckled, "We can work on your technique when you're better. I will come by today to see you."

"Thanks for checking on me."

thirty:

After Commander Red spoke with Presscott he went to speak with Jonathan. Commander Red had a speech prepared for Jonathan but when he walked in the cell Jonathan asked, "Are we being recorded?"

"No."

"I will answer any question that you have for me truthfully after you check out this address."

"What is this about?"

"Most importantly, I'm in love with my wife and I want us back. Also, two people are being held hostage there, when they are rescued and brought here, I will tell everything to everyone."

Commander Red studied Jonathan's face for a moment trying to see truth in his words. It was the urgency in his entire demeanor that made the decision for Commander Red. He then spoke into his radio and said, "Nikko and Sean please respond."

A short moment passed and they both responded.

"Go for Nikko."

"Go for Sean."

"CC yesterday."

One said 10-4, while the other said in route.

All three of the gentlemen got to the Command

Center at the same time. Commander Red escorted them to his office and closed the door.

"I have been given a potential lead on something we may really need. Jonathan has disclosed an address that is holding two people hostage. He says once the two people are back here safely he will tell us everything."

"Sir you believe him why?" Sean asked.

"Because he does love Presscott," Nikko said with a simple smile.

"Sir I am going to follow your command but I need it to go on record that I absolutely do not agree with this chain of action."

"Duly noted and thank you for your honesty." Commander Red needed to act fast. So he said, "Nikko grab Juan as your second on this op. I want audio and visual comms up before you leave the compound. I will be in your head the entire time."

"Yes sir." Nikko said very focused.

"No body bags." Commander Red demanded.

Nikko saluted and walked out of the office.

The radio crackled and Nikko said, "Juan garage yesterday."

"10-4," Juan responded.

"Sean you are now my number two in the compound. I need the family along with Remmington, Detective

Brendel and Director Copeland in the Combat Situation Room a.s.a.p." Commander Red was giving orders as solutions was flooding his mind

----

Once everyone was in the C.S.R. Commander Red briefed everyone on what was about to be seen and heard.

Director Copeland and Detective Brendel immediately got on their phones and started putting back up together for Nikko.

"Nikko." Director Copeland said his name out loud, "Can you hear me?"

Nikko's voice came back loud and clear, "Yes Sir. Go with your traffic."

"Watch for a black suburban to flash its lights. He will pull up on your left side and the passenger window will be down. The passenger will hold up a sign with two names, Erick and Danny. Erick is driving, Danny is the passenger. Danny is my lead so he needs to patch into your comm. He will hold up his radio and you do the same. You two have to hold steady for five seconds for synchronization to take place. You will then have a crew of fifteen extra men at your disposal." Director Copeland explained.

"10-4. Thank you Sir." Nikko responded.

The C.S.R. got quiet again and then Presscott began to ask the question, "So Commander why are you taking the word of Jonathan?"

"When I went in to speak to him earlier this morning, he spoke with great urgency."

"Why was the urgency a determining factor?"

"My gut screamed inside of me to follow the lead."

"Did you tell me that the way Jonathan was brainwashed, it is according to Military standards?"

"Yes."

"How do you know that?"

"Jonathan was my study subject."

Presscott's jaw tensed. Everyone in the room just watched and listened to the two of them silently. Then she began to yell at the top of her lungs asking a question to everyone, "ARE THERE ANY MORE DAMNED SECRETS IN THIS FAMILY THAT I NEED TO KNOW ABOUT!"

No one spoke and no one moved.

"Yall betta speak now or forever hold your peace and I mean forever damn it." Presscott's voice was low and calm.

Still no one spoke or moved.

Presscott activated the intercom in the middle of the conference table and said, "This is Dr. Presscott Elizabeth

Ellington Chandler I want the detainee in the C.S.R. yesterday."

An unknown male voice responded immediately, "Yes ma'am. ETA two mics."

Commander Red cleared his voice to speak but Presscott cut him off with, "Don't speak unless I address you."

The room remained still until Jonathan was delivered.

"What is your name?" Presscott asked the private that delivered Jonathan.

"Gerald Author Winston ma'am," he answered proudly with a salute.

"At ease Mr. Winston," she said smiling, "I just want to thank you for moving so swiftly."

"You are welcome. Is there anything else before I return to post?" He was so excited that Dr. Chandler now knew his name.

"Yes, please unshackle the detainee." Her demand was calm and polite. "I would also like for you to stay in here."

"Now Jonathan, who are the two individuals being held at this address?" Presscott asked Jonathan with no Emotion present.

I will only talk to Commander Red in private."

Jonathan answered.

"Nina, I want the third and fourth rib on the right side. Nonny I apologize that you are here for this." Presscott entered into a calmness that had everyone a little nervous inside.

Nina was so excited because she actually wanted to kill Jonathan. She took off her shoes and socks and ran up to Jonathan on her toes. She jumped in the air, she kicked Jonathan's right arm out of the way with her right foot and broke his third and fourth ribs with the heel of her left foot.

Jonathan let out a yell of excruciating pain. Once Jonathan was able to control his cry Presscott said, "That is the only question that I have for you. I have the ability to make your situation a lot worse..." Presscott's words were cut off by Nikko's voice filling the room.

"ETA fifteen mics, do we know who we are rescuing yet?"

"I'm working on it, give me just a moment." Presscott said.

Hannah and Remmington were sitting the closest to Jonathan when he mumbled the two names.

Remmington's hand slapped the table and the two friends looked at each other, "Did you hear what I heard?" Remmington asked Hannah.

"I did." Hannah answered.

The two friends scrambled to the floor so they could really hear what Jonathan was saying.

"Jonathan baby say it again, we didn't hear you." Hannah prompted sweetly.

They balanced themselves on one another and put their ears almost in Jonathan's mouth and he said again, "Kiki Combs and Corbin Wolfe, both victims." Then Jonathan passed out from pain.

Hannah repeated out loud what Jonathan said to Nikko.

Then Remmington said to Presscott, "If we find out this boy is playing with my emotions, I swear to God Scottie."

"Detective Brendel," Hannah began talking as she got off of the floor. "I need your people to locate the Combs family. Once Nikko has Kiki then the family needs to be brought here."

"Mr. Winston please take Jonathan to the medical suite. Let them know that his third and fourth ribs on the right need to be set. And inform them that two more patients are coming but we don't know the extent of their injuries."

Mr. Winston proudly went into action.

thirty-one:

There was a buzz in the room of controlled chaos, calls were being made, orders were being given and then Juan's voice was heard, "Commander Red, this location is the Ellington Tower satellite office in Gwinnett. There is a high volume of civilians."

"Juan..." Mudear cut him off, "It's Mudear. This building actually belongs to me. I want you to drive around to the north east side of the building. There is a keypad, the code is 03201969." Then she looked at Director Copeland as she said, "I am going to see if I can get you a real time infrared satellite image. I can walk you through the building." Mudear turned and winked her eye at Presscott. "Is it possible to get a Cherry Coke?" Mudear asked and they all chuckled.

"Commander Red," he looked toward Director Copeland, "We are going to need an unmarked bus at this site that can handle the two vics for transport. Can you handle that?

"Yes Sir." Director Copeland answered.

"I will take care of the escort." Detective Brendel chimed in.

Mudear walked over to a wooden panel and pressed

the corner of it. A smart monitor dropped with satellite images on it, she put the address of her building in a dialog box. She whispered, "There's my baby."

"Naomi," Mudear called out for Nonny.

"Yea." Nonny answered.

"Do you know how to operate remote control cars?"

"I'm the mother of two boys, the grandmother of three grandsons and my husband is an architect. What do you think?" They both laughed.

Mudear pulled down another monitor and activated the location. "Okay," Mudear handed Nonny a list of codes. "Here we go Naomi. Input these codes and you will have complete control of the cameras on the inside. Now once we get our envoy on the screen then we will switch. As of right now everyone is coded red for enemy. The software on this program will start weeding out civilians and they automatically turn yellow. Remmington is going to hand me pics of Corbin and Kiki so I can color code them blue, they are packages. Nikko and company will be coded green for friendlies. Are you with me so far?"

"Yep I gotcha, let's bring our babies home." Nonny high fived Mudear while everyone in the room watched them with amazement.

Mudear stood up and locked in both screens a little

above waste high. Then she asked, "Nina is your family fluent in Spanish?"

"Yes ma'am." Nina answered.

"Who translates better, you or your mother?" Mudear asked as she walked over to get her Cherry Coke.

"My mother," Nina answered with pride.

"Okay, Juanita are you up to translating for me?" Mudear asked.

"If that's what you need, I most certainly am." Juanita was happy she got to be a part of the working mothers underground.

"Thank you," Mudear said. "Let me explain," she dropped another monitor and kept it in a seated position. She activated the screen and said, "You will be watching the sound waves of the communications for Nikko and Juan. If the sound wave turns orange, then you say out loud 'coms down' and click the big red square that says DOWN. Nikko and Juan can no longer hear us, they can only hear you speaking Spanish. If the sound wave turns orange that means Ellington is listening to the communication and to keep our babies safe we now speak Spanish."

"I understand Elizabeth. Can I have a Cherry Coke too?" Juanita asked smiling.

"When did your mother become military savvy?"

Remmington asked Hannah.

"Probably when Scottie became a Free Runner." Hannah laughed.

Presscott assessed that the C.S.R. was in good hands with the mothers so she slipped out. She needed to clear her head so she walked over to the common area and sat on a picnic table nursing a Cherry Coke.

thirty-two:

"Mudear," Nikko's voice was heard out loud, "we are at the north east entrance.

"Okay, give me just a moment. I'm double checking to make sure you are clear. My goal is to get you all in and out in fifteen minutes. Move on my go. Remmington I need an infinite loop of the back gate closed, camera 12A" Mudear was in her element.

Remmington walked over to Nonny's monitor and clicked the screen twice and said, "Looped."

"Nikko go." Mudear said.

The envoy began to move.

Nikko once you all get in the gate, turn your vehicles around to exist. Keep your engines running two people stay behind.

Mudear and Nonny switched monitors, Mudear explained to Nonny in quick whispers what she was looking out for.

"Nikko walk to the end of the building to your right. The loading dock should be opened, the code to the freight elevator is 0320#" Mudear looked at her monitor and started to move cameras around in the building.

"Bus is on location and ready for departure." Commander Red said out loud.

"Escorts are in position, ready for departure." Detective Brendel said out loud.

"Guys go to the first floor." Mudear directed.

"Remmington I need you on a monitor."

Remmington dropped a monitor panel on the opposite side of the room. She hacked into Mudear's system and pulled up the most current blue prints.

"Rem, hold the freight between the first and second floor for a moment. Lock all the doors and opaque all the glass on 1 sector 3D."

"Done," Remmington responded quickly.

"Manually unlock the freight. Gentlemen try the first office on your left," Mudear directed.

"Guys, looks like there are two bodies hog tied on the floor." Nonny said in shock.

"Gentlemen at the gate bring in the bus and escorts to the loading dock." Director Copeland said out loud.

"Boys you are clear to move," Mudear said.

The room got disturbingly still and quiet. The images on the screen were gut wrenching and provoked an ungodly anger.

Once Nikko and Juan cleared the building Remmington unlocked freight 1, sector 3D. When the entire envoy was cleared, Remmington reversed the infinity loop on camera 12A.

Halcyon looked around the room for Presscott and did not see her so she said, "Good job everyone. Mudear I was very impressed with your 'commando' skills. Who knew? Remmy I did not know you were so tech savvy. When Nikko and Juan get back let's make sure we give them too much love.

Detective/Director may we have at least a week before we have to give statements? I will get with Presscott to schedule a debrief time, so look for a memo from me this week. I am going to find a comedy to watch tonight if anyone wants to come over and watch. This has been a bitter sweet ending today, and I am sure this is the first of many so let's go get distracted."

Mudear, Nonny and Juanita went walking through the compound not talking but the three of them wanted to be together and there they saw Presscott sitting on the picnic table.

"Butterfly you all right baby?" Nonny asked as she got to her first.

"Yes ma'am, I'm fine." Presscott answered.

"Were you in the C.S.R. to see the outcome?" Mudear asked.

Presscott took a deep breath because she did not know if she wanted to hear this yet, then she answered,

"No ma'am."

"Well," Juanita began, "you would have been so proud of your mother. She ran that operation like it was second nature to her. The Director, Detective and Commander took orders from your mother, it was awesome."

They all laughed a nervous laugh and Presscott understood that something was not being spoken. So she touched Mudear's hand and asked softly, "Was Jonathan telling the truth?"

Mudear moved extremely close to Presscott and said, "Yes baby, he was telling the truth. We got them out undetected no casualties. Both of them are alive but unconscious. The Combs family is in route and we are still looking for Corbin's next of kin."

Presscott let out a sigh of relief and asked, "This has just begun, hasn't it?"

Juanita placed her hand on Presscott's stomach and said, "We the mamas, we got this."

All four of them toasted their Cherry Coke bottles and said, "To the mamas."

THE END.

Thank you for taking out the time to read my book, I truly appreciate it.
If you have any correspondence to the book please direct it to:
Justicelovecreativity@gmail.com

See you at the second installment.